A FEW NICE WORDS

"Extremely readable!"
— Sierra Club *Traveler's Guide*

"Looking for a weekend retreat or a long vacation? This book...is a must!"
— Colorado Historical Society

"Looking for a bed and breakfast in Colorado in which to stay? If it's not listed in *Absolutely Every* Bed & Breakfast in Colorado (*Almost),* it probably doesn't exist."
— Rocky Mountain News

"What sets this book apart from other guidebooks is it's objectivity and...its thoroughness."
— *Springs Magazine*

"It's just the facts, ma'am, in this refreshing guide. Quick reference and easy reading. What a pleasure. You want to head for Colorado on a B&B excursion..."
— Gail Greco, Author
Tea-Time at the Inn, and
Secrets of Entertaining from America's Best Innkeepers

"The book is wonderful."
— Noel Wilson
Something Special B&B
Winter Park, CO

"We do appreciate being in your book, for it is very well done. When it first hit the bookstores, we purchased several for our Bed & Breakfast and our guests have used it constantly."
— Lee & Kathy Bates
Ouray 1989 House B&B

"Thanks for all your help in making the B&B industry successful and prosperous. Keep up the good work!!!"
— Holden House 1902 B&B Inn
Colorado Springs, CO

Absolutely Every*
BED & BREAKFAST
in
COLORADO
almost

TONI KNAPP, EDITOR

Special Contributor:
CHARLES HILLESTAD

Rebecca Riese, Editorial Assistant

The Rocky Mountain Series

Second Edition

The Rockrimmon Press, Inc.
Colorado Springs

Cover photograph of Hallett Peak over Dream Lake
Rocky Mountain National Park
by Jim Osterberg, Estes Park, CO

Maps by Carl Bandy

Title design by Connie Crandall

Typesetting by Service Typographers

Printed by Industrial Printers of Colorado, Inc.

Library of Congress Cataloging-in-Publication Data

Knapp, Toni
    Absolutely every° bed & breakfast in Colorado °almost /
Toni Knapp. — 2nd ed.
        p.   cm. — (The Rocky Mountain series)
    ISBN 1-882092-08-2
    1. Bed and breakfast accommodations—Colorado—Guide-
books. 2. Colorado—Guidebooks. I. Title. II. Title:
Absolutely every° bed and breakfast in Colorado °almost.
III. Series.
TX907.3.C6K53   1992
647.9478803—dc20   92-8158
                                                               CIP

Printed in the United States of America

A B C D E F G

THE ROCKY MOUNTAIN SERIES

ABSOLUTELY EVERY BED & BREAKFAST IN
ARIZONA (*Almost)*

ABSOLUTELY EVERY BED & BREAKFAST IN
COLORADO (*Almost)*

ABSOLUTELY EVERY BED & BREAKFAST IN
NEW MEXICO (*Almost)*

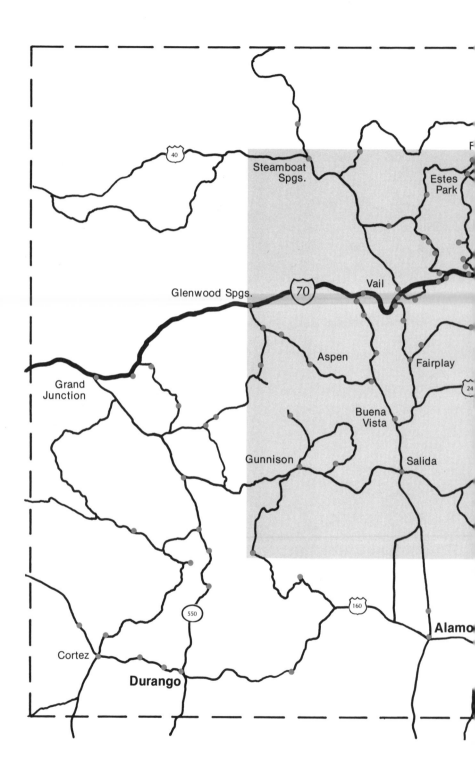

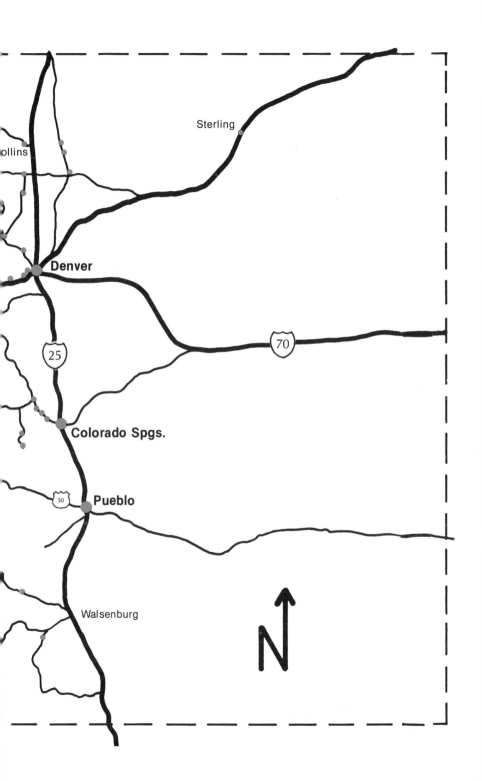

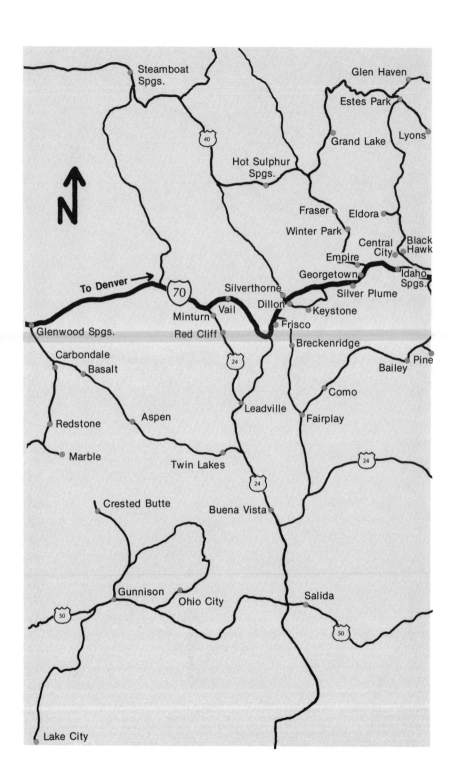

CONTENTS

Lark Bunting

INTRODUCTION

Bed and Breakfast, that great European tradition, has finally come of age in America, spreading rapidly across the country and away from the old strongholds of the east and west coasts. In Colorado, the crown jewel of the Rocky Mountains, it is an emerging force in the hospitality industry. Indeed, it is a bountiful one.

Imagine being able to choose from 287 B&B's in 101 cities and towns from Alamosa to Yellow Jacket, including the great resort areas of Aspen/Snowmass, Vail/Beaver Creek, Crested Butte, Winter Park, Steamboat Springs, Keystone, Breckenridge and Telluride!

Here in this magnificent state, B&B accommodations are not just the proverbial quaint, romantic or rustic. They're also **adventurous** (and sometimes charmingly odd). For example, you can stay in B&B trout, pinto bean and environmental farms, llama ranches, remote mountain cabins, ski lodges, railroad cars (this is true), big city mansions, Victorian inns, Anasazi archaeological sites, and famous, genuine castles.

Every one of the B&B accommodations listed in this book is a "true" B&B; that is, breakfast is included in the price of the room.

Complete information about each B&B was provided in writing by the innkeepers, and their responses are on file with the publisher.

To ensure the integrity of this guide, **Innkeepers did not pay to be listed.**

Our guide is organized in a clear, friendly format that avoids codes, symbols and endless narrative. But we have included little thumbnail sketches of each geographical area to help our readers know where they are headed.

All Reservation Service Organizations (RSO's) and trade associations listed in this directory were given the opportunity to list their member B&B's. Those that responded did so voluntarily, and did not pay to be included.

The room rates given in this book were current as of press time. But this is a volatile industry. Closings and changes in prices and ownership occur regularly. That's why it's advisable to **always** call ahead. Dropping in is chancy and seldom welcomed.

We wish to make very clear that the editor, contributing authors, and Rockrimmon Press, Inc., make no warranty, implied or specific, about the operations or policies of Bed & Breakfast establishments,

1

RSO's, or trade associations mentioned in this book. *Absolutely Every°
Bed & Breakfast in Colorado (°Almost)* is not about the bed and
breakfast industry. It is intended as a helpful resource for the B&B
traveler.

One thing is certain. Your Bed & Breakfast experiences in Colorado will surely change the way you travel. We welcome your comments, suggestions, B&B news, and fan letters...and we wish you a
Rocky Mountain High!

Toni Knapp

Rocky Mountain Big Horn Sheep

COLORADO: AN AMERICAN CLASSIC

*I*t seems fitting that Colorado was the inspiration for our "other" national anthem, "America the Beautiful." Katherine Lee Bates wrote her famous poem after gazing in wordless rapture, from atop Pikes Peak, at the expanse of mountains and plains spread before her. The "purple mountain majesties" referred to are quite literally Pike's Peak and Colorado's Front Range. The "fruited plain" and "amber waves of grain" are the farm and ranch lands spread along an incredible curtain wall of 14,000 foot peaks. Colorado represents what America is all about.

It can be said there are actually seven Colorados, each separate and distinct in geography and attractions.

DENVER

The smallest of the Colorados, this "Queen City of the Plains" is big in every other aspect. For thousands of visitors each year, a major stop in discovering the state is its capitol, a teeming metropolitan area surrounded by mountains and with a nearly perfect high, dry and sunny four- season climate. Contrary to popular myth, neither Denver or the rest of the state is buried in snow ten months a year. Low humidity and 300 days of sunshine see to that.

Denver is not all modern buildings. With 24 historic districts and more than 250 officially designated historic buildings, the city is history personified, and one of the mining capitols of the old west.

Some of the best museums in the country are here. The Museum of Natural History, with its dinosaurs, dioramas and giant IMAX Theater, is the fourth largest in the nation. The U.S. Mint is here. The Art Museum and Center for the Performing Arts rival any in the country. Denver is also home to the Denver Grand Prix, Broncos Football Team, and National Western Stock Show. And it is the gateway to some of the best skiing in the world with 28 ski areas and ten world-class resorts.

NORTH CENTRAL

Three-fourths of all the area in America above two miles is in Colorado. That's right. That includes 53 peaks above 14,000 feet.

Some of the most awe-inspiring are the white-capped jewels of Rocky Mountain National Park. Its pristine lakes, spring wildflowers, the aspen gold of autumn, and abundant wildlife, make this a spectacular place to visit year-round through its major gateway, Estes Park.

Gold is very much a presence almost everywhere in the North Central area. Many of the towns in this sector were built as a result of the state's early gold and silver mining fever. Georgetown, Silver Plume, Central City and Black Hawk are today lively "ghost towns" that preserve Colorado's past.

Culture is alive and well in this state. Music, dance, theater and film festivals can be found everywhere, from opera in Central City to Shakespeare in Boulder. The University of Colorado in Boulder, and Colorado State University in Fort Collins are centers for cultural events, also.

NORTHWEST

Here is Colorado's alpine kingdom. When winter's champagne powder falls, it is transformed into a skiers' paradise.

Consistently ranked best in the nation, 17 of the 28 ski areas are here, including Vail, Aspen/Snowmass, Keystone, Steamboat Springs, Breckenridge and Copper Mountain.

The nation's only five-star dude ranch is here as well. And, would you believe sailing at nearly two miles above sea level? You can at Lake Dillon.

Most towns with "Springs" in their names have a mineral water source. Steamboat Springs alone has 157 separate hot springs within its boundaries. Glenwood Springs has the biggest natural hot springs pool in the world. For an unforgettable steamy experience, try it on a cold winter night.

This diverse section of Colorado is rich in forests, rivers, gemstones, dinosaur fossils, fruit orchards and vineyards. The rich and famous are plentiful, too, in Aspen and Vail. Anyone who dreams of castles will find a very real and historic one in Redstone, once a barony owned and built by a coal magnate for his workers.

And near Grand Junction, The Grand Mesa, the largest flat top mountain in the world, has been designated a National Monument.

SOUTHWEST

Rich in its diverse beauty, the geography in southwestern Colorado is fascinating. Here is the magnificent Black Canyon of the Gunnison, a chasm 50 miles long, 2900 feet deep, and a National Monument. From the quarry in the town of Marble came the stone used in the Lincoln Memorial and Washington Monument. Mesa Verde National Park and the Anasazi Cliff Dwellings are near Cortez, and Colorado's largest National Historic District is in Lake City. Durango offers many opportunities for alternative modes of travel. The Durango-Silverton Narrow Gauge Train and its steam engine will take you over 45 miles of breathtaking scenery between the towns of the same name. Or if hiking is your bent, try the 469-mile trail that stretches from Durango to Denver and traverses 7 national forests, 6 wilderness areas, 5 river systems and 8 mountain ranges. Of course, mountain bikers all know that this is the home of the famous Iron Horse Bicycle Classic and The World Mountain Bike Championships.

Summer in Telluride, the festival capitol of the U.S., is a continuous celebration of everything from jazz and blue grass to film, mushrooms and hang gliding. Skiing there isn't bad, either.

In Crested Butte, the old and the new blend together in this world-class ski resort and historic mining town.

All together, this amazing southwest area has more than eight million acres of national forests and other accessible public lands.

SOUTH CENTRAL

South central Colorado encompasses the agricultural beauty of the San Luis Valley, the incredible Great Sand Dunes National Monument, the white water rapids of the Arkansas River, Florissant Fossil Beds National Monument, the historic towns of Cripple Creek and Victor, and the nation's highest suspension bridge across the Royal Gorge.

Colorado Springs, the state's second-largest city, is a growing cultural and industrial center. Here in the shadow of Pikes Peak is the Air Force Academy, NORAD, and the U.S. Olympic Training Complex.

You can have a breathless driving experience at 13,186 feet over Mosquito Pass. And as for mountains, Chaffee County has the greatest number of mountain peaks over 14,000 feet, known as the magnificent Collegiate Range.

SOUTHEAST AND NORTHEAST

The entire eastern half of Colorado sweeps over the Great Plains, sometimes called the High Plains, from the Pawnee Prairie down across fields of winter wheat, giant cattle ranches, truck farms and prairie dog towns.

An indelible mark has been placed over the region by the roaming South Platte River, immortalized in James Michner's *Centennial*. "A mile wide and an inch deep" back when fur traders stalked the area, it was the original route for commerce in the state.

While the northeast and southeast quadrants are dominated by the open plains, the southern portion has a distinctive Spanish flavor which evolved from its 300-year-old Spanish land grants.

Pueblo, the state's third largest city, is a growing economic and multicultural base in the region.

No matter where you go in our fair state, you will find what you are looking for, if what you are looking for is unequaled recreation, unsurpassed views, friendly natives, great entertainment, and the perfect Bed & Breakfast.

Charles Hillestad

Charles Hillestad is a Denver attorney specializing in real estate and business law. He is active in the B&B industry nationally, and is Associate Editor of Inn Times. He and his wife, Ann, own and operate the Queen Anne Inn in Denver, CO.

6

BED & BREAKFAST IN COLORADO: EVERYTHING YOU NEED TO KNOW
Charles Hillestad

*E*arly forms of this overnight accommodation concept, sometimes called "tourist homes," have been around for decades and are particularly common in Europe. In this country, they represent a fairly recent phenomenon that has grown beyond the borders of New England and spread across the nation. Growth has been so rapid, there may be as many as 20,000 existing today, a number triple that of 1985 and ten times that of 1980, according to *Condé Nast Traveler*. That growth has been a direct result of the traveling public's apparent desire for intimate accommodations emphasizing distinctiveness, personalized service and hospitality.

Many B&B's in Colorado and the Rocky Mountain Region, where their numbers have skyrocketed, have been acknowledged as among the finest in the world. Literally thousands of articles have been written on what charming, "escapist" places to stay they represent. However, much confusion remains as to exactly what a B&B is and which type is "best." The bed & breakfast accommodations listed in this book can be defined as being in the following categories: Host Home (or Homestay), B&B Inn, Country Inn, Lodge, B&B Hotel, and Guesthouse.

"B&B" is a generic term encompassing a wide variety of accommodations. Definitions vary, but B&B's tend to be relatively small. In this book, the term B&B will apply to those establishments under fifty rooms, ranging from a secluded mountain cabin or gingerbread Victorian, to a full service hotel.

Some B&B's are fancy and expensive. Some are funky and low cost. Many are historic. Others are of recent vintage. All are delightfully unique. Their only unifying theme is that a proper breakfast is included in the price, something far more than donuts and instant coffee.

The key to eliminating mixups and potential unpleasant surprises is to understand the several distinct categories of B&B's. Although the following explanations are only approximate, they still should give some guidance in that regard.

A **Guesthouse** is an entire unit—a small house, cabin, or possibly a condominium for rent and qualifies as a B&B when breakfast is delivered each day. Here there is usually not quite the same opportunity for interaction with the hosts or other guests as there is in other types of B&B's. That can be viewed as an advantage if anonymity is desired. Guesthouses are usually included with Homestays if they are deemed to be B&B's.

A **Host Home** (or **Homestay**) normally is a B&B. A designation as a Host Home is not a reflection on quality or professionalism. Some Host Homes are among the finest, most professionally run places that can be found. A Host Home is primarily a private home where the resident owner rents out one to five spare bedrooms. This often means private baths may be the exception rather than the rule but, as with all B&B's, the percentage of private baths to rooms is increasing. Staff seldom exceeds two or three people counting the owners. Government licensing and inspection is rare, especially so on homes with three rooms or less. An outside sign or advertising is also rare, though not necessarily in all cases.

A **B&B Inn** is the most rapidly growing category and may today represent a majority of the B&B's. It operates as a full time business and provides the customary conveniences of the hospitality industry. Licensing and signage are the rule. The boundary line between Inn and Host Home is somewhat fuzzy. Typically, B&B Inns have six to twelve rooms, larger staffs and a higher percentage of private baths.

A **Country Inn** is much like a B&B Inn and the terms are often interchangeable. The difference is that many Country Inns are located in rural areas, and often have restaurants where lunch and/or dinner is available.

Lodges are often Country Inns located in wilderness areas. Although not all Lodges are B&B's, the ones listed in this book qualify as such because breakfast is included.

B&B Hotels, sometimes called Historic Hotels or Small Hotels, are sort of full service B&B's with such extras as concierge, bars, restaurants, shops, or room service. Our designation of B&B Hotels include those with between 25 and 50 rooms.

Other Things to Know. It is important to note that the above definitions have absolutely nothing to do with quality. They are objective criteria to help you distinguish between rough groupings, such as the difference between hotels and host homes.

In determining the category of a particular B&B, the name of the establishment and the opinion of the owner should not be deciding factors. Consider size and services offered only. Anything else would be too subjective. Consequently, XYZ House could be a Historic Hotel. ABC Hotel could be an Inn. Look at the objective criteria when evaluating a potential place to stay. There is no "best" category, only what is best for you personally. The important thing to remember is to ask questions about the price, room, bed, bath, breakfast, amenities, "rules of the house," and any restrictions. Most B&B's prohibit smoking, for example.

Check and see if pets and children are permitted, and if the hot tub and swimming pool are actually operational. Don't assume air conditioning is present, or that locks, phones or TV's are available either (but why would one go on a romantic escape and then watch TV?).

If you want to find out about quality, rely on word of mouth from those who have stayed there, rely on the reviewer guidebooks you have come to trust, rely on panels of judges who give awards to innkeepers or on the standards, inspections and ratings systems developed for B&B's, such as those of the American B&B Association, the International Inn Society, Mobil, the American Automobile Association, Innovations, or Ziggat.

A B&B experience is one of the most pleasant a traveler can ever have. But to avoid surprises, it never hurts to ask questions in advance.

"Listing" B&B Guidebooks. Now that you know what B&B's are, how do you find them? The most complete source is a listing guide-book. Keep in mind, though, that the descriptions in many such books often come from the innkeepers who pay to have the information included. This is not so in *Absolutely Every* * *Bed & Breakfast in Colorado* (*Almost*). Innkeepers have no final control over what is said. And, it provides extra information on things such as awards, honors, reviews and ratings, which can be found nowhere else.

"Critic" B&B Guidebooks. A second good way to find B&B's is a critic or reviewer guidebook. In this type of book, someone has ventured an independent opinion on various B&B's. They function like movie reviews. If your taste coincides with the reviewer's, you will probably enjoy the experience.

The only B&B's included in these kinds of books are ones which tickled the fancy, or met the minimum standards, of the authors. Usually, no one has paid to be rated. You may disagree with the opinion expressed, but at least it is the editor's own thoughts uninfluenced by advertising or other revenue from the inns. If the B&B you are investigating has not been critiqued, that does not mean it is not deserving.

Normally, the B&B's are personally inspected by the writing staff, although that is not the case with every book. In any event, the following recommended critic guidebooks feature, at least in part, Colorado. Remember not to use a book that is more than two years old.

American Bed & Breakfast Association. *Inspected, Rated and Approved B&B's*, Midlothian, VA : ABBA.

Birnbaum, Steven. *Birnbaum's United States*, Boston: Houghton Mifflin.

Caughey, Bruce and Winstanley, Dean. *The Colorado Guide: Landscapes, Cityscapes, Escapes*, Golden, CO: Fulcrum.

Kennedy, Doris. *The Guide to the Recommended Country Inns of the Rocky Mountain Region*, Chester, CT: Globe Pequot Press.

Layton, Marie T. *Colorado B&B Guide*, Golden, CO: Fulcrum, 1990.

Levitin, Jerry. *Bed & Breakfast American Style*, New York: Harper & Row.

———. *Country Inns and Back Roads*, New York: Harper & Row.

Metzger, Stephen. *Colorado Handbook*, Chico, CA : Moon Publications.

Soule, Sandra W. *America's Wonderful Little Hotels & Inns*, New York: St. Martin's.

Other useful B&B Guidebooks worth checking include:

AAA Colorado/Utah Tourbook, Heathrow, FL : American Automobile Association.

Barnes, Rik and Nancy. *Complete Guide to American B&B's*, Gretna LA: Pelican Publications.

Buzan, Norma. *B&B North America*, Bloomfield Hill, MI : Betsy Ross Publications.

Frommer's Denver, Boulder, & Colorado Springs, New York: Prentice Hall.

Hitchcock & Lindgren. *The Recommended Country Inns, Lodges and Historic Hotels of the Midwest and Rocky Mountain States*, Chester, CT : Globe Pequot.

Lanier, Pamela. *Complete Guide to B&B Inns & Guest Houses*, Oakland, CA : Lanier Publishing International.

Mobil Travel Guide Southwestern U.S., Chicago: Rand McNally.

Sturni, Barbara and Dane, Suzanne. *Featherbeds and Flapjacks*, Washington, D.C. : National Trust for Historic Preservation.

B&B Trade Associations. Trade associations are not automatically reservation services, although many do make direct reservations. Normally, a true trade association is a non-profit organization whose principal purpose is to help and promote its member B&B's. Again, we have tried to indicate which B&B's in this book are members of the following trade associations.

Distinctive Inns of Colorado (formerly Colorado Inn Association) is a non-profit trade association composed exclusively of highly rated B&B Inns and Country Inns. For a free copy of its brochure, send a stamped, self-addressed envelope to:

> Distinctive Inns of Colorado
> PO Box 10472
> Colorado Springs, CO 80932-1472
> (800) 866-0621

Bed & Breakfast Innkeepers of Colorado, another statewide non-profit trade association, also publishes a directory of its inspected and approved member Inns. For a copy of their directory send a self-addressed, long envelope and $1.00 to:

Bed & Breakfast Innkeepers of Colorado
1102 W. Pikes Peak Ave., Dept. RP
Colorado Springs, CO 80904
(800) 746-2242 (BBIC)

For directories of B&B's in ski and resort areas, contact:

Bed & Breakfast Assn. of Vail/Ski Areas
Kathy Westerberg
PO Box 491
Vail, CO 81658
(303) 949-1212
(800) 748-2666

Bed & Breakfast of Winter Park
PO Box 800
Winter Park, CO 80482
(303) 726-5360

Two other trade associations with Colorado membership are:

Professional Assn. of Innkeepers International
Jo Ann M. Bell & Pat Hardy
PO Box 90710
Santa Barbara, CA 93190
(805) 965-0707

Tourist House Association
R.D. 2, Box 355A
Greentown, PA 18426
(717) 857-0856

Colorado B&B Reservation Service Organizations. Also known as RSO's, reservation services represent a useful alternative to guidebooks. They can also supplement information in the books, saving you a lot of research effort.

As with most RSO's, B&B's pay to belong, as well as a commission fee for each room rented through an RSO. Sometimes, guests may pay a small surcharge as well when booking through an RSO.

RSO's are basically similar to travel agencies. They are particularly useful if the traveler desires Host Homes. Since most of these maintain a low profile and do not advertise, RSO's are the only way to find them.

The Key to a successful experience with an RSO is to ask questions. Tell them exactly what you are looking for and quiz them thoroughly on the places they recommend. Ask what their standards are for selecting places to be listed by their service. Ask about costs, check-in times, cancellation policies, air conditioning, etc., and about the policies on children, smoking and pets. Ask about private baths, the furniture, the breakfast, the view, the hosts. Remember, a B&B is not a "cookie cutter" motel chain. Do not automatically assume anything.

RSO's should not be confused with Trade Associations discussed above. They have different purposes.

Where possible, the listings in this book indicate whether a particular B&B is served by one of the following RSO's:

Bed & Breakfast Rocky Mountains
Frank & Cheryll Carroll
906 S. Pearl
Denver, CO 80209
(303) 744-8415
(800) 733-8415

Central Reservations
Central City, CO 80427
(303) 278-7859

Durango Area Chamber Resort Assn.
PO Box 2587
Durango, CO 81302
(303) 247-0312

The Higher Elevations Co.
PO Box 457
Lake City, CO 81235
(303) 944-2644

Off the Beaten Path
109 E. Main
Bozeman, MT 59715
406-586-1311

Ouray Central Reservations
PO Box 727
Ouray, CO 81427
(800) 255-0009

Small Luxury Hotels
337 S. Robertson Blvd.
Suite 202
Beverly Hills, CA 90211
800-525-4800

Summit Central Reservations
PO Box 446
Dillon, CO 80435
(303) 468-6222

Telluride Central Reservations
666 W. Colorado
Telluride, CO 81435
(800) 525-3455

Four national RSO's worth mentioning will help you find an appropriate RSO elsewhere.

B&B Reservation Services World Wide, Inc.
PO Box 39000
Washington, DC 20016
(800) 842-1486

B&B: The National Network
PO Box 4616
Springfield, MA 01101

Innres
7203 Arlington Ave.
Riverside, CA 72503
(800) 777-1460

Treadway Reservations Service
180 Summit Ave.
Montvale, NM 07645
(800) 873-2392

Formal Ratings Systems: B&B's in this book may have been rated by the following national organizations:

American B&B Assn.
1407 Huguenot Rd.
Midlothian, VA 23113
ATTN: Sarah W. Sonke
(804) 379-2222

American Automobile Assn.
1000 AAA Dr.
Heathrow, FL 32746-5063

International Inn Society
50 Kenney Place
PO Box 1912
Saddle Brook, NM 07662
(201) 652-1484

Mobil Travel Guides
PO Box 7600
Chicago, IL 60680

If you have questions or comments about the information in this section, please write to Charles Hillestad, 2151 Tremont Place, Denver, CO 80205. Please include a stamped, self-addressed envelope for a reply.

Armed with all this information, you should have a great time in your quest for your own perfect B&B. Have fun!

BED & BREAKFAST

DIRECTORY

ALAMOSA

One of the state's most productive agricultural areas in the center of the San Luis Valley, 200 miles southwest of Denver, via I-25 and Hwy. 160. The gateway to the Great Sand Dunes National Monument, home of the Alamosa National Wildlife Refuge for migratory birds, and Adams State College. Browse in the Rio Grande Art Market, and check out the Gallery & Artists Home Tour in November.

COTTONWOOD INN BED & BREAKFAST AND GALLERY

123 San Juan Ave.   Alamosa, CO 81101   (719) 589-3882
George Sellman & Julie Mordecai-Sellman, Resident Owners

LOCATION	Corner of San Juan Ave. & 2nd, 3 blocks from Main St. (Hwy. 160)
OPEN	All Year
DESCRIPTION	1908 2-Story Craftsman Bungalow Antique furnishings
NO. OF ROOMS	4 w/private bath 2 w/shared bath
RATES	PB/$60-75 SB/$50-54 Reservation/cancellation policy Inquire about minimum stay on special weekends
CREDIT CARDS	Diner's Club, MasterCard, Visa
BREAKFAST	Full gourmet, served in dining room Sack lunches available
AMENITIES	Complimentary refreshments, ice water in rooms, robes, TV/VCR & stereo in parlor
RESTRICTIONS	No smoking. No pets (resident dog)
REVIEWED	*America's Wonderful Little Inns & Guesthouses* *The Colorado Guide* *Fodor's Colorado* *Frommer's Colorado* *Recommended Country Inns of the Rocky Mountain Region*
RSO	B&B Rocky Mountains
MEMBER	American B&B Assn. B&B Innkeepers of Colorado Colorado Hotel/Motel Assn. Professional Assn. of Innkeepers International

ALLENSPARK

In the Roosevelt National Forest, 16 miles south of Estes Park and 7 miles west of Lyons, via Hwy. 7.

ALLENSPARK LODGE

PO Box 247   184 Main   Allenspark, CO 80510   (303) 747-2552
Mike & Becky Osmun, Resident Owners   FAX: (303) 747-2811

LOCATION	16 mi. south of Estes Park on Hwy. 7
OPEN	All Year
DESCRIPTION	1933 Lodge Rustic furnishings
NO. OF ROOMS	5 w/private baths 9 w/shared baths
RATES	PB/$59.95-74.95 SB/$39.95-54.95 Reservation/cancellation policy
CREDIT CARDS	MasterCard, Visa
BREAKFAST	Continental plus, served in common room Lunch & dinner available
AMENITIES	Hot tub/sauna, complimentary refreshments, meeting facilities
RESTRICTIONS	No smoking. No pets
REVIEWED	*Recommended Country Inns of the Rocky Mountain Region*
RSO	B&B Rocky Mountains
RATED	Mobil 2 Stars

19

ARVADA
(DENVER)

A thriving suburb 15 miles west of Denver, with its own Center for the Arts and Humanities.

ON GOLDEN POND BED & BREAKFAST

7831 Eldridge   Arvada, CO 80005   (303) 424-2296
Katharina Kula, Resident Owner

LOCATION	Suburban Denver, 5 mi. northwest of I-70, Exit 266
OPEN	All Year
DESCRIPTION	1977 Contemporary 2-Story Brick On 10 acres w/natural fishing pond & floating gazebo Eclectic furnishings
NO. OF ROOMS	5 w/private baths
RATES	$50-80 Reservation/cancellation policy
CREDIT CARDS	American Express, MasterCard, Visa
BREAKFAST	Full, served in dining room, guestrooms, country kitchen, or on deck
AMENITIES	Swimming pool, hot tub w/whirlpool, robes, TV/radio/phone/ jacuzzi tubs/fireplaces in rooms, verandas, late afternoon pastries & coffee, bicycles, fishing on property, handicapped access, small meeting facilities
RESTRICTIONS	No smoking. Pets outdoors only (resident dog & cat)
RSO	B&B Rocky Mountains
MEMBER	B&B Innkeepers of Colorado

THE TREEHOUSE

6650 Simms   Arvada, CO 80004   (303) 431-6352
Mailing address: 6600 Simms, Arvada, CO 80004
Sue Thomas, Owner

LOCATION	2 mi. north of I-70 at Ward Rd. exit
OPEN	All Year
DESCRIPTION	1960 Chalet In 10-acre forest Antique furnishings, brass beds & handmade quilts
NO. OF ROOMS	5 w/private baths
RATES	$49-89 Reservation/cancellation policy
CREDIT CARDS	MasterCard, Visa
BREAKFAST	Full, served in dining room
AMENITIES	Robes, fireplaces, TV/radio, complimentary refreshments, common area w/fireplace, use of kitchen/laundry facilities, handicapped access, small meeting facilities
RESTRICTIONS	No smoking. No pets
RSO	B&B Rocky Mountains

ASPEN

Historic silver mining boom town and now a world-class resort. From Denver, 200 miles west via I-70 to Glenwood Springs and Hwy. 82. Or try a summer-only shortcut over Independence Pass. Alpine skiing on four mountains, summer's Aspen Music Festival, Gold Medal fishing in the Roaring Fork River, aspen-viewing in the fall, and celebrity-watching all year. Or head to Ashcroft/Toklat & visit the sled dogs at Krabloonik's Kennels.

ALPINE LODGE

1240 E. Cooper   Aspen, CO 81611   *(303) 925-7351*
Christina Martin, Resident Owners   *FAX: (303) 925-7351*

LOCATION	On Hwy. 82, 1/2 mi. east of Gondola, 1/4 mi. from center of town
OPEN	All Year
DESCRIPTION	1890 Bavarian Guesthouse w/Cabins Bavarian furnishings
NO. OF ROOMS	Main house: 4 w/private baths 3 w/shared baths Cabins: 4 w/private baths
RATES	PB/$40-83 SB/$35-58 Reservation/cancellation policy
CREDIT CARDS	American Express, MasterCard, Visa
BREAKFAST	Continental, served in dining room Dinner available
AMENITIES	Down comforters, hot tub, TV/radio in lobby, some rooms w/TV/radio, 1 cabin w/kitchenette, complimentary beverages
RESTRICTIONS	Smoking & pets in cabins only. Resident dog & cat
REVIEWED	*The Colorado Guide* *Recommended Country Inns of the Rocky Mountain Region*
RSO	Aspen Central Resort Travel Aspen Ski Tours

THE ASPEN BED & BREAKFAST LODGE

311 West Main St.   Aspen, CO 81611   (303) 925-7650   (800) 362-7736
Jim Lowe, Manager   *FAX: (303) 925-5744*

LOCATION	6 blocks from center of Aspen
OPEN	All Year
DESCRIPTION	Contemporary B&B Hotel, river rock facade Contemporary furnishings
NO. OF ROOMS	38 w/private baths
RATES	$79-119 Reservation/cancellation policy
CREDIT CARDS	American Express, Discover, MasterCard, Visa
BREAKFAST	Full, served in dining room
AMENITIES	Hot tub, swimming pool, TV/phones, refrigerators in rooms, complimentary beverages, small meeting facilities
RESTRICTIONS	No pets
RSO	Aspen Central Reservations
MEMBER	Colorado Hotel/Motel Assn.
RATED	AAA 3 Diamonds Mobil 3 Stars

23

CHRISTMAS INN
BED & BREAKFAST LODGING

232 W. Main St.   Aspen, CO 81611   (303) 925-3822
Larry Mautz, Owner   (800) 521-4055

LOCATION	Center of Aspen, on Main St. between 1st & 2nd Sts.
OPEN	All year. B&B Thanksgiving-Mid April only
DESCRIPTION	Contemporary Alpine B&B Hotel
NO. OF ROOMS	22 w/private baths
RATES	$50-136 Reservation/cancellation policy 3-night minimum during holidays & special event weekends
CREDIT CARDS	No
BREAKFAST	Full, served in dining room
AMENITIES	Sauna/jacuzzi, cable TV/phones in rooms, maid service, complimentary Apres Ski in winter
RESTRICTIONS	No pets
RSO	Aspen Central Resort Travel
RATED	Mobil 1 Star

HEARTHSTONE HOUSE

134 E. Hyman   Aspen, CO 81611   *(303) 925-7632*
Irma Prodinger, Resident Owner   *FAX: (303) 920-4450*

LOCATION	Corner of Aspen & Hyman Sts., center of Aspen
OPEN	Dec. 15 to April 10 & June 10-Sept. 10
DESCRIPTION	1961 Frank Lloyd Wright Scandinavian furnishings
NO. OF ROOMS	17 w/private baths
RATES	Dbl/$158-225 Sgl/$96-158 Reservation/cancellation policy 3-night minimum
CREDIT CARDS	American Express, MasterCard, Visa
BREAKFAST	Full, served in dining room
AMENITIES	Sauna, whirlpool, robes, TV/phone/radio in rooms, turndown service, Austrian herbal steam bath, complimentary afternoon tea
RESTRICTION	No smoking. No pets. Inquire about children
REVIEWED	*America's Wonderful Little Hotels & Inns*
RSO	Aspen Central Resort Travel
MEMBER	Colorado Hotel & Motel Assn.
RATED	Excellent, Premier Rating Systems, Aspen

HEATHERBED MOUNTAIN LODGE

1679 Maroon Creek Rd.   *PO Box 530   Aspen, CO 81611*   *(303) 925-7077*
Neal Henley, Manager   *(800) 356-6782*   *FAX: (303) 925-6120*

LOCATION	Across street from Aspen Highlands Ski Area, 2 mi. outside of town, on the way to the Maroon Bells
OPEN	All Year (Closed part of Oct. & April)
DESCRIPTION	1960 A-Frame European & Country furnishings
NO. OF ROOMS	18 w/private baths
RATES	Seasonal Rates: $49-275 Reservation/cancellation policy
CREDIT CARDS	MasterCard, Visa
BREAKFAST	Continental plus, served in sunroom
AMENITIES	Swimming pool, hot tub/sauna, down comforters, TV/phone in rooms, fireplace in one room, microwave in lobby, ski storage, laundry room, valet service, complimentary refreshments & full après ski, fishing rods in summer
RESTRICTIONS	Smoking limited. No pets. No incoming phone calls after 7 p.m.

HOTEL LENADO

200 S. Aspen St.   Aspen, CO 81611   (303) 925-6246   (800) 321-3457
Jayne Poss, General Manager   FAX: (303) 925-3840

LOCATION	Center of Aspen
OPEN	All Year
DESCRIPTION	1983 3-Story Contemporary Rustic Lodge
NO. OF ROOMS	19 w/private baths
RATES	Summer/$135-185 Winter/$120-335 Reservation/cancellation policy
CREDIT CARDS	American Express, Diner's Club, MasterCard, Visa
BREAKFAST	Full gourmet, served in breakfast room or guestroom
AMENITIES	Hot tub, robes, TV, phones, library, screening room w/VCR, bar, complimentary evening hors d'oeuvres, turn-down service, chocolates on pillows, down comforters, daily maid service, meeting room, concierge, whirlpool baths, heated ski-boot lockers, many rooms have wet bars, refrigerators, balconies, wood-burning stoves
RESTRICTIONS	Smoking limited. No pets
REVIEWED	*America's Wonderful Little Hotels & Inns* *Colorado B&B Guide* *The Colorado Guide* *Guide to the Recommended Country Inns*
MEMBER	Colorado Hotel & Motel Assn. Distinctive Inns of Colorado
RATED	Mobil 4 stars

INDEPENDENCE SQUARE HOTEL

404 S. Galena St.   Aspen, CO 81611   *(303) 920-2313*
National/800-882-2582   Colorado/800-443-2582   FAX: (303) 920-2020
Julie Adams, Resident Manager

LOCATION	Center of Aspen, on the Mall
OPEN	All Year
DESCRIPTION	Victorian B&B Hotel French Country furnishings
NO. OF ROOMS	28 w/private baths
RATES	Seasonal Rates: $95-285 Reservation/cancellation policy Inquire about minimum stays
CREDIT CARDS	MasterCard, Visa
BREAKFAST	Continental plus buffet, served in atrium lounge
AMENITIES	Rooftop jacuzzi/sundeck, complimentary use of The Aspen Club, Cable TV, phones, wet bar/refrigerators in rooms, individual ski lockers, airport transportation, turndown service, air conditioning
RESTRICTIONS	Smoking limited. No pets
REVIEWED	*America's Wonderful Little Hotels & Inns*
MEMBER	Colorado Hotel & Motel Assn.

INVERNESS LODGE

122 E. Durant   Aspen, CO 81611   (303) 925-8500   FAX: (303) 925-8789
Kimberly Hay, Manager

LOCATION	On the corner of Durant Ave. & Aspen St., 1 block from Aspen Mt. 1A Lift
OPEN	All Year
DESCRIPTION	1960 European
NO. OF ROOMS	22 w/private baths

RATES	$39-185
	Reservation/cancellation policy
	3-night minimum, 7-night during Christmas
CREDIT CARDS	Discover, MasterCard, Visa
BREAKFAST	Continental plus, served in lobby
AMENITIES	Hot tub, cable TV/phone in rooms, apré ski
RESTRICTIONS	No smoking. No pets
RSO	Aspen Central Reservations
MEMBER	Aspen Lodge Assn.

LITTLE RED SKI HAUS

118 E. Cooper   Aspen, CO 81611   (303) 925-3333
Irene Zydek, General Manager

LOCATION	Center of Aspen. 1-1/2 blocks from Aspen Mt. ski lift
OPEN	All Year
DESCRIPTION	1890's 2-story Victorian
	Authentic period furnishings
NO. OF ROOMS	3 w/private baths 17 w/shared baths
RATES	Summer: PB/$68 SB/$20-48
	Winter: PB/$82-112 SB/$27-82
CREDIT CARDS	American Express, MasterCard, Visa
BREAKFAST	Summer/continental Winter/full
	Served in dining area
AMENITIES	Winter: Complimentary aprés ski party, afternoon soup &
	crackers, picnic, coffee/tea all day
RESTRICTIONS	No smoking. No pets
REVIEWED	*The Colorado Guide*
	Recommended Country Inns of the Rocky Mountain Region

MOUNTAIN HOUSE BED & BREAKFAST

905 E. Hopkins   Aspen, CO 81611   (303) 920-2550
FAX: (303) 920-3440, Ext. 532
P.J. Sullivan & Syd Devine, Resident Managers

LOCATION	4 blocks east of Hyman Ave. Mall, on corner of Hopkins & West End
OPEN	All Year
DESCRIPTION	1987 Contemporary rustic Southwestern furnishings
NO. OF ROOMS	24 w/private baths 6 suites
RATES	Seasonal Rates: $35-300 Reservation/cancellation policy
CREDIT CARDS	American Express, Diner's Club, Discover, MasterCard, Visa
BREAKFAST	Summer/continental plus Winter/full Served in dining room
AMENITIES	Jacuzzi in lodge, all rooms have cable TV/phones, refrigerator, 11 rooms w/wet bars, most rooms have decks, fireplaces in lobby & lounges, complimentary aprés ski in winter, coffee/tea all day, ski lockers
RESTRICTIONS	No pets
RSO	B&B Rocky Mountains
MEMBER	Colorado Hotel and Motel Assn.

SARDY HOUSE

128 E. Main St.   Aspen, CO 81611   (303) 920-2525   (800) 321-3457
Jayne Poss, Manager   *FAX: (303) 925-3840*

LOCATION	Center of Aspen
OPEN	Thanksgiving to mid-April & mid-June to mid-October
DESCRIPTION	1892 Restored Victorian
NO. OF ROOMS	14 w/private baths 6 suites w/private baths
RATES	Summer/$160-375 Winter/$160-550
	Reservation/cancellation policy
CREDIT CARDS	American Express, Diner's Club, MasterCard, Visa
BREAKFAST	Full gourmet, served in dining room or guestrooms
	Gourmet dinner available in restaurant
AMENITIES	Heated pool, sauna, jacuzzi, robes, TV & phones in rooms, whirlpool bath in all rooms/suites, some rooms w/antique bath, bar, turn-down service, daily maid service, room service, concierge service, meeting room
RESTRICTIONS	Smoking limited. No pets
MEMBER	Distinctive Inns of Colorado
REVIEWED	*America's Wonderful Little Hotels & Inns*
	Colorado B&B Guide
	The Colorado Guide
	Recommended Country Inns of the Rocky Mountain Region
	The Official Guide to American Historic Inns
RATED	Mobil 4 Stars

SNOW QUEEN VICTORIAN BED & BREAKFAST

124 E. Cooper St.   Aspen, CO 81611   (303) 925-8455/6971
Norma Dolle & Larry Ledingham, Owner/Managers   FAX: (303) 925-8455

LOCATION	On corner of Cooper & Center Sts., center of Aspen
OPEN	All Year
DESCRIPTION	1889 Victorian Victorian furnishings
NO. OF ROOMS	4 w/private baths 2 w/shared bath
RATES	PB/$35-115 SB/$30-105 Reservation/cancellation policy Inquire about minimum stay
CREDIT CARDS	American Express, MasterCard, Visa
BREAKFAST	Continental plus, served in kitchen
AMENITIES	Outdoor hot tub, lounge w/fireplace & TV, TV/phones in rooms, weekly après ski party in winter
RESTRICTIONS	No pets
RSO	Aspen Central Resort Travel

STAPLETON SPURR BED & BREAKFAST

1370 Owl Creek Rd.   PO Box 98   Aspen, CO 81612   (303) 925-7322
Sam & Elizabeth Stapleton, Resident Owners   FAX: (303) 925- 7322

LOCATION	4 mi. west of Aspen, 1-1/4 mi. off Hwy 82, just behind airport, on top of hill
OPEN	June-Oct. & Nov.-April (Inquire)
DESCRIPTION	1968 Ranch Country furnishings

NO. OF ROOMS	4 w/2 shared baths
RATES	$50-60 Reservation/cancellation policy 2-night minimum, 1-week minimum during Christmas
CREDIT CARDS	MasterCard, Visa
BREAKFAST	Continental, served in dining room or on outside deck
AMENITIES	TV/radio/phone & fireplace in living room, complimentary refreshments occasionally
RESTRICTIONS	No smoking. No pets (resident cats & dogs). Children over 3
RSO	Aspen Chamber Resort Assn.

ULLR LODGE BED & BREAKFAST

---

520 W. Main   Aspen, CO 81611   (303) 925-7696
Anthony Percival, Resident Owner   FAX: (303) 920-4339

LOCATION	Corner of Main & 5th Sts., west end of Aspen, residential area. 10 min. walk to town
OPEN	All Year
DESCRIPTION	1986 Swiss Chalet Contemporary furnishings
NO. OF ROOMS	10 w/private baths
RATES	$50-55 Reservation/cancellation policy
CREDIT CARDS	American Express, MasterCard, Visa
BREAKFAST	Summer/continental Winter/full Served in dining room
AMENITIES	Heated outdoor pool, hot tub, game room, ping pong, complimentary afternoon tea in winter
RESTRICTIONS	No smoking. No pets
RSO	Aspen Central Resort Travel Aspen Ski Tours
RATED	AAA 2 Diamonds Mobil 1 Star

AULT

A rural farming area in the northeast plains, 16 miles east of Fort Collins, and 11 miles north of Greeley, at the edge of Pawnee National Grasslands.

THE ADAMS HOUSE

200 B Street   PO Box 459   Ault, CO 80610   (303) 834-1587
Jim & Sue Adams, Resident Owners

LOCATION	4 mi. north of Eaton. 2 blocks south & 1 block west of intersection of Hwys. 85 & 14
OPEN	All Year
DESCRIPTION	1907 2-Story Victorian Farmhouse w/wrap around porch & gingerbread trim Traditional furnishings
NO. OF ROOMS	2 w/private baths
RATES	Sgl/$30 Dbl/$35 Reservation/cancellation policy
CREDIT CARDS	No
BREAKFAST	Full, served in formal dining room, or in garden gazebo in summer
AMENITIES	Radio in rooms, landscaped garden w/pond, waterfalls & gazebo, complimentary refreshments upon arrival, meeting facilities, limited handicapped access
RESTRICTIONS	No smoking. No pets
REVIEWED	B&B U.S.A.

AVON
(VAIL/BEAVER CREEK)

What could be better? Only 12 miles west of Vail and 2 miles west of Beaver Creek, via I-70 & Hwy. 6.

MOUNTAIN RETREAT

Through Reservation Service Only:
PO Box 491   Vail, CO 81658   (303) 949-1212   (800) 748-2666

LOCATION	2 mi. west of Beaver Creek
OPEN	November 1-April 15
DESCRIPTION	1981 Southwestern Southwestern furnishings
NO. OF ROOMS	1 w/private bath
RATES	$85-125 Reservation/cancellation policy
CREDIT CARDS	MasterCard, Visa
BREAKFAST	Full, served in dining room
AMENITIES	Hot tub/sauna, robes, TV/radio/phone in rooms, complimentary refreshments
RESTRICTIONS	No smoking. No pets (resident cat). No children
RSO	B&B Assn. of Vail/Ski Areas

OUTDOORSMAN

Through Reservation Service Only:
PO Box 491   Vail, CO 81658   (303) 949-1212   (800) 748-2666

LOCATION	In Avon, 1/2 mi. west of Beaver Creek
OPEN	November 1-April 15
DESCRIPTION	Contemporary Townhome Contemporary furnishings
NO. OF ROOMS	1 w/private bath
RATES	$50-85 Reservation/cancellation policy
CREDIT CARDS	MasterCard, Visa
BREAKFAST	Full, served in dining room
AMENITIES	Robes, TV/radio in rooms, complimentary refreshments
RESTRICTIONS	No smoking. No pets (resident dog). No children
RSO	B&B Assn. of Vail/Ski Areas

BAILEY

On the South Platte River and a prime spot for trout fishing, 35 miles southwest of Denver on Hwy. 285.

GLEN-ISLE RESORT

573 Old Stagecoach Rd.   PO Box 128   Bailey, CO 80421   (303) 838-5461
Gordon & Barbara Tripp, Resident Owners

LOCATION	1.7 mi. west of Bailey on Hwy. 285
OPEN	B&B June 1-Sept. 15 only Cabins open all year
DESCRIPTION	1900 Slab & Shingle Lodge w/Cabins Restaurant & Antique Shop On 160 acres National Historic Register
NO. OF ROOMS	14 w/shared baths
RATES	$40-50 Reservation/cancellation policy
CREDIT CARDS	No
BREAKFAST	Full, served in dining room Other meals available in restaurant Cookouts, picnics, porch buffets by request
AMENITIES	Fireplaces in cabins, children's playground, ping-pong, billiards, shuffleboard, sing-a-longs, square dancing, horseshoes, movies, bingo games, library, trout fishing, horseback riding, meeting facilities
RESTRICTIONS	Extra charge for pets (Resident dogs)
REVIEWED	*The Colorado Guide*

BASALT

Small town between Aspen and Glenwood Springs, 160 miles west of Denver via I-70 and Hwy. 82, near the Roaring Fork and Frying Pan rivers. Windsurfing at Reudi Reservoir is an eyeful.

ALTAMIRA RANCH

6878 Highway 82   Basalt, CO 81621   (303) 927-3309
Martha Waterman, Resident Owner

LOCATION	160 acres on Roaring Fork River, 1 mi. south of Basalt
OPEN	All Year
DESCRIPTION	1906 Rebuilt Ranch House Eclectic furnishings
NO. OF ROOMS	2 w/shared bath
RATES	$40-60 Reservation/cancellation policy 3-night minimum during holidays
CREDIT CARDS	No
BREAKFAST	Full, served in dining area
AMENITIES	Stocked fishing pond, antique shop
RESTRICTIONS	No smoking. No pets (resident dog). Children over 6
REVIEWED	*Colorado B&B Guide*
RSO	B&B Rocky Mountains
MEMBER	B&B Innkeepers of Colorado

COZY LOG HOME

246 Hooks Lane   Basalt, CO 81621   (303) 927-4125
Jeanie Perrow, Resident Owner

LOCATION	20 mi. west of Aspen/Snowmass, just off Hwy. 82
OPEN	April-November
DESCRIPTION	1875 Remodeled Hand-Hewn Log House Oak furnishings & fur floors
NO. OF ROOMS	1 w/private bath 1 w/shared bath
RATES	PB/$40-50 SB/$35-45 Reservation/cancellation policy
CREDIT CARDS	No
BREAKFAST	Continental, served in dining area Vegetarian dinner available on request
AMENITIES	Wood-burning stove, phone, use of kitchen/refrigerator, laundry facilities, dog house & fenced area for pets
RESTRICTIONS	No smoking. Pets outside only (resident cat)
RSO	B&B Rocky Mountains

SHENANDOAH INN

0600 Frying Pan Rd.   PO Box 578   Basalt, CO 81621   (303) 927-4991
Bob & Terri Ziets, Resident Owners

LOCATION	.6 mi. east of Basalt on Frying Pan River
OPEN	All Year (Closed end of Apr. & 1st of Nov.)
DESCRIPTION	1968 Renovated Country w/large deck On 2 riverfront acres Southwestern & country furnishings
NO. OF ROOMS	4 w/2 shared baths
RATES	$50-100 Reservation/cancellation policy
CREDIT CARDS	MasterCard, Visa
BREAKFAST	Full, served in dining room Dinner & catering available
AMENITIES	All rooms overlook river, radio in rooms, cable TV/VCR in family room, complimentary refreshments
RESTRICTIONS	No smoking. No pets. Children over 12
RSO	B&B Rocky Mountains
MEMBER	B&B Innkeepers of Colorado

BEAVER CREEK
(VAIL)

Sometimes called "The Last Resort", Vail's sister resort offers up the new Grouse Mountain Express High-Speed Quad for advanced skiers, multitudes of Pro-Am ski and golf competitions (Gerald Ford lives here), a wealth of summer festivals & celebrations, and the usual celebrity-watching. Or indulge in a little romantic luxury with a snowcat-driven sleigh ride to dinner at Beano's Cabin (sigh!). From Vail, 10 miles west on I-70, and 3 miles south on Exit 167.

ELK VIEW

Through Reservation Service Only:
PO Box 491   Vail, CO 81658   (303) 949-1212   (800) 748-2666

LOCATION	At Beaver Creek Mountain, ski-in & ski-out
OPEN	All Year
DESCRIPTION	1988 European Eclectic furnishings
NO. OF ROOMS	3 w/private baths
RATES	Summer/$75-80 Winter/$100-125 Reservation/cancellation policy 2-night minimum in winter
CREDIT CARDS	MasterCard, Visa
BREAKFAST	Full, served in dining room
AMENITIES	Hot tub/sauna, robes, TV/radio in rooms, complimentary refreshments
RESTRICTIONS	No smoking. No pets. No children
RSO	B&B Assn. of Vail/Ski Areas

BELLVUE

A small community 20 miles northwest of Fort Collins via Hwys. 287 & 14, on the nationally-designated wild & scenic Cache La Poudre River.

GYPSY TERRACE BED & BREAKFAST

4167 Poudre Canyon   Bellvue, CO 80512   (303) 224-9389
Linda & Vern Rasmussen, Resident Owners

LOCATION	On Hwy. 14, 4 mi. west of Hwy. 287, north of Bellvue
OPEN	All Year
DESCRIPTION	1910-1940 Restored Elevated Ranch On the Cache la Poudre River Antique & eclectic furnishings w/oak floors & vaulted beamed ceilings
NO. OF ROOMS	2 w/private baths
RATES	$55-60 Reservation/cancellation policy
CREDIT CARDS	MasterCard, Visa for reservations only
BREAKFAST	Full, served in dining room Sack lunches & bedtime snack available on request
AMENITIES	Wood stove in great room, deck, covered parking, complimentary refreshments
RESTRICTIONS	No smoking. No pets. No children

BEULAH

Beautiful, scenic southwestern area in Beulah Valley, on the eastern edge of the Wet Mountains, 25 miles west of Pueblo, via I-25 and Hwy. 78.

BEULAH HOUSE

8733 Pine Dr.   Beulah, CO 81023   (719) 485-3201
Harry & Ann Middelkamp, Resident Owners

LOCATION	1 mi. south of Beulah
OPEN	All Year
DESCRIPTION	Early 1900's Spanish Lodge On 25-acre wildlife park Spanish & Native American furnishings
NO. OF ROOMS	Main House: 3 w/private baths Guest House: 1 suite w/private bath 3 w/shared bath
RATES	PB/$75 & up SB/$50 Reservation/cancellation policy
CREDIT CARDS	MasterCard, Visa
BREAKFAST	Full or continental, served in dining room, guestrooms or on patio
AMENITIES	Swimming pool (103°) & pool house w/stocked refrigerator, hot tub in main house, greenhouse w/hot tub, sauna, robes, 1 room w/fireplace, TV/radio in rooms if requested, phone available, all room w/stocked bars, complimentary refreshments, meeting facilities, handicapped access, Chapel w/courtyard & fountain
RESTRICTIONS	No smoking. No pets (resident dog, cats, & wildlife). No children
REVIEWED	*The Colorado Guide*

KK RANCH & CARRIAGE MUSEUM

8987 Mountain Park Rd.   Beulah, CO 81023   (303) 485-3250
Kay Keating, Resident Owner   (800) 258-5866

LOCATION	On Mountain Park Rd., just off south Pine Dr. in Beulah Valley
OPEN	All Year
DESCRIPTION	1870 Homestead house Rustic Antique furnishings
NO. OF ROOMS	3 w/shared baths
RATES	$35-45 Reservation/cancellation policy
CREDIT CARDS	Accepted when using RSO
BREAKFAST	Continental plus, served in dining room
AMENITIES	Fireplace in one room, TV in common area, kitchen privileges on request, horse-drawn carriage for weddings or special events, meetings in summer only
RESTRICTIONS	No smoking. Inquire about pets (resident dogs, cats, horses, donkeys & mules)
REVIEWED	*The Colorado Guide* *Great American Guest Houses*
RSO	B&B Rocky Mountains

Black Hawk

Victorian mining town and National Historic District, 29 miles west of Denver via Hwys. 6 & 119, 1 mile from Central City.

Bed & Breakfast Inn at Blackhawk

251 Main   PO Box 258   Black Hawk, CO 80422   (303) 582-5235
Bobbi Thompson, Manager

LOCATION	Center of town, within walking distance to Casinos
OPEN	All Year
DESCRIPTION	Contemporary 3-Story House Contemporary furnishings
NO. OF ROOMS	10 w/private baths
RATES	$60-70 Reservation/cancellation policy
CREDIT CARDS	MasterCard, Visa
BREAKFAST	Full, served in dining room
AMENITIES	Recreation room w/cable TV, free parking
RESTRICTIONS	No smoking. No pets. No children
RSO	Central Reservations

Chase Mansion Bed & Breakfast

201 Chase Gulch   PO Box 599   Black Hawk, CO 80422   (303) 582-0112
Debra Start, Resident Owner   *FAX: (303) 277-0646*

LOCATION	1st left on Historic Chase Gulch, north of intersection of Hwys. 279 & 119. Close to Gaming District
OPEN	All year

DESCRIPTION	1869 Victorian Mansard
	Antique furnishings
NO. OF ROOMS	1 w/private bath 2 w/shared bath
RATES	PB/$45-85 SB/$45-85
	Reservation/cancellation policy
CREDIT CARDS	Inquire
BREAKFAST	Continental, served in dining room
AMENITIES	Robes, TV/radio in rooms, VCR & tapes, books & games, use of kitchen, laundry service, childcare, small meeting facilities, business services available, bicycle, camera & camcorder rentals
RESTRICTIONS	None. Resident dog, cat & ghost

THE SHAMROCK INN

351 Gregory St.   PO Box 137   Black Hawk, CO 80422-0137
Herb & Jeri Bowles, Resident Owners   *(303) 582-5513*

LOCATION	Within walking distance to Gaming District, on shuttle route to Central City
OPEN	All Year
DESCRIPTION	1870's 2-Story Victorian
	Some antique furnishings
NO. OF ROOMS	3 w/private baths
RATES	$60
	Reservation/cancellation policy
CREDIT CARDS	No
BREAKFAST	Full, served in dining room
AMENITIES	On-site parking
RESTRICTIONS	No pets. No children
REVIEWED	*The Colorado Guide*

BOULDER

Home of the University of Colorado, the National Center for Atmospheric Research, and (world class) cycling capitol of the U.S. This high-tech, upscale city lies 30 miles northwest of Denver via Hwy. 36 (Boulder Turnpike) and 40 miles south of Estes Park. Check out the Pearl Street Pedestrian Mall, the Summer Shakespeare Festival and Music Festival, the Bolder Boulder Memorial Day 10K run, and just about everything else.

THE ALPS BOULDER CANYON INN

PO Box 18298   38619 Boulder Canyon Dr.   Boulder, CO 80302
John & Jeannine Vanderhart, Resident Owners   (303) 444-5445

LOCATION	In Boulder Canyon, 1.8 mi. west of downtown .
OPEN	All Year
DESCRIPTION	1870 Remodeled (1991) Country Inn English country furnishings
NO. OF ROOMS	12 w/private baths
RATES	$80-160 Corporate & weekly rates available Reservation/cancellation policy
CREDIT CARDS	American Express, Diner's Club, Discover, MasterCard, Visa
BREAKFAST	Full, served in dining room Special meals available
AMENITIES	All rooms w/double jacuzzi tubs & steam showers, antique wood-burning fireplaces, TV/radio/phones, down comforters & pillows in most rooms, robes, complimentary afternoon & evening refreshments, meeting facilities, handicapped access
RESTRICTIONS	No smoking. No pets (resident dog & cats)

THE BOULDER VICTORIA HISTORIC BED & BREAKFAST

1305 Pine St.   Boulder, CO 80302   (303) 938-1300   FAX: (303) 938-1435
Jacki Myers, Manager   Kristen Peterson, Asst. Manager

LOCATION	2 blocks from Pearl Street Mall
OPEN	All Year
DESCRIPTION	1895 Renovated Victorian Period antique furnishings
NO. OF ROOMS	7 w/private baths
RATES	$88-150 Reservation/cancellation policy
CREDIT CARDS	American Express, Diner's Club, MasterCard, Visa
BREAKFAST	Continental plus, served in dining room or guestrooms Gourmet picnic lunches & catering available
AMENITIES	Steam showers, robes, cable TV/radio/phone in rooms, private patios or balconies, down comforters, complimentary afternoon refreshments, espresso bar, FAX & copier facilities, concierge service, wedding/meeting/reception facilities, limousine, limited handicapped access
RESTRICTIONS	No smoking. No pets. Children over 8, $25 additional
AWARDS	Historic Boulder Preservation Award, 1991
REVIEWED	*The Colorado Guide*
MEMBER	Professional Assn. of Innkeepers International

BRIAR ROSE

2151 Arapahoe Ave.   Boulder, CO 80302   (303) 442-3007
Margaret & Bob Weisenbach, Resident Owners

LOCATION	Corner of 22nd St. & Arapahoe, adjacent to CU campus & Naropa Institute
OPEN	All Year
DESCRIPTION	1892 Queen Anne Victorian Main House & Carriage House Antique furnishings National Historic Register
NO. OF ROOMS	9 w/private baths
RATES	Summer/$65-105 Winter/$63-98
CREDIT CARDS	American Express, Diner's Club, MasterCard, Visa
BREAKFAST	Continental plus, served in dining room, guest rooms, or on sun porch
AMENITIES	Robes, TV/radio & phone in rooms, complimentary tea trays, fresh flowers, chocolates on pillows, 2 rooms w/fireplaces, common room w/fireplace
RESTRICTIONS	Smoking restricted. No pets (resident dog)
REVIEWED	*B&B American Style* *Colorado B&B Guide* *The Colorado Guide* *Country Inns & Backroads* *Frommer's Denver, Boulder, & Colorado Springs* *Recommended Country Inns of the Rocky Mountain Region*
RSO	B&B Rocky Mountains
MEMBER	B&B Innkeepers of Colorado Distinctive Inns of Colorado
RATED	Mobil 2 Stars

GUNBARREL GUEST HOUSE

6901 Lookout Rd. Boulder, CO 80301 (303) 530-1513
Rose Wittig, Manager   FAX: (303) 530-4573

LOCATION	7 mi. north of Boulder via Diagonal Hwy. 119
OPEN	All Year
DESCRIPTION	1986 Contemporary Contemporary furnishings
NO. OF ROOMS	13 w/private baths
RATES	$90-100 Reservation/cancellation policy
CREDIT CARDS	American Express, Diner's Club, MasterCard, Visa
BREAKFAST	Continental plus, served in dining room
AMENITIES	Green house w/jacuzzi, robes, TV/radio/phones/fireplaces in rooms, complimentary refreshments, meeting facilities for 45 persons, outdoor courtyard suitable for small social events
RESTRICTIONS	No pets

THE MAGPIE INN ON MAPLETON HILL

1001 Spruce St. Boulder, CO 80302   (303) 449-6528
Scott Coburn, Owner & Nancy Raddatz, Manager FAX: (303) 444-7968

LOCATION	Corner of 10th & Spruce in Mapleton Hill Historic District, 2 blocks from Pearl St. Mall
OPEN	All Year
DESCRIPTION	1899 Restored Denver Square Brick Victorian Victorian furnishings
NO. OF ROOMS	5 w/private baths 2 w/shared bath

RATES	PB/$98 SB/$68-78 Reservation/cancellation policy
CREDIT CARDS	American Express, MasterCard, Visa
BREAKFAST	Continental plus, served in dining room
AMENITIES	Fireplaces, TV/radio in rooms, phones in rooms, 2/w balconies, phones on request, fireplace in Great Room, games, books, complimentary refreshments, meeting facilities, limited handicapped access, off-street parking
RESTRICTIONS	Smoking limited. No pets
RSO	B&B Rocky Mountains

Paintbrush Ranch & Pottery

14497 Gold Hill Rd.   Boulder, CO 80302   (303) 459-3547
Beryl Knauth, Owner   Regine Cazabon, Resident Manager

LOCATION	17 mi. west of Boulder, up Sunshine Canyon, Boulder County Rd. 52
OPEN	All Year
DESCRIPTION	1960 Log Lodge & Campground Resort On 100 acres
NO. OF ROOMS	2 w/private baths 2 w/shared bath Outdoor accommodations: 5 tipis, 1 yurt (nomadic tipi), 3 domed tent cabins
RATES	Lodge/$59 Yurt/$59 Outdoor facilities/$12-36
CREDIT CARDS	MasterCard, Visa
BREAKFAST	Continental plus, served in dining hall Other meals available for special events
AMENITIES	Swimming pool, lounge, stage, meeting facilities, horseback riding, fishing in stocked pond, volleyball, horseshoes
RESTRICTIONS	No smoking. Resident dogs, cat & horses
MEMBER	Colorado Campground and CabinResort Assn.

PEARL STREET INN

1820 Pearl St.   Boulder, CO 80302   (303) 444-5584   (800) 232-5949
Mark Holmes, Manager   FAX: (303) 444-6494

LOCATION   Center of Boulder, 3 blocks south of Pearl St. Mall

OPEN   All Year

DESCRIPTION   1893 Victorian w/1985 addition & central courtyard
                    Contemporary Victorian furnishings

NO. OF ROOMS   7 w/private baths

RATES   Sgl/$58-73   Dbl/$68-113
                    Corporate & weekly rates available
                    Reservation/cancellation policy

CREDIT CARDS   American Express, MasterCard, Visa

BREAKFAST   Full, served in dining room, guestrooms or courtyard
                    Lunch & dinner available upon request

AMENITIES   Phone/TV/fireplaces in rooms, turndown service, conference
                    & banquet rooms, courtyard, full bar, concierge service,
                    complimentary afternoon refreshments, reserved parking,
                    handicapped access

RESTRICTIONS   None

AWARDS   Best of Boulder Award

REVIEWED   *America's Wonderful Little Hotels & Inns*
                    Frommer's Denver, Boulder, & Colorado Springs
                    Recommended Country Inns of the Rocky Mountain Region

THE SANDY POINT INN

6485 *Twin Lakes Rd.*   *Boulder, CO 80301*   *(303) 530-2939*
Juaneta Miller, Resident Manager   *(800) 322-2939*   *FAX: (303) 530-9101*

LOCATION	3-1/2 mi. northeast of Boulder via Diagonal Hwy. 119, 2 blocks east of 63rd St.
OPEN	All Year
DESCRIPTION	1984 Contemporary Contemporary furnishings
NO. OF ROOMS	29 studio suites w/private baths & kitchenettes
RATES	$63-73 Reservation/cancellation policy
CREDIT CARDS	American Express, Diner's Club, Discover, MasterCard, Visa
BREAKFAST	Continental plus, served in dining area
AMENITIES	TV/radio, phone, microwave/refrigerator/dishes in room, complimentary use of health club, laundry facilities, conference room, limited handicapped access, catering available
RESTRICTIONS	Small pets only
RATED	AAA 2 Diamonds Mobil 1 Star

BRECKENRIDGE
(SUMMIT COUNTY)

Beautifully restored 130-year-old Victorian gold rush mining town and National Historic District. Now a major 3-mountain ski area and summer resort with outstanding music festivals, and part of a paved bike path system that ends (or begins) in Vail. Ullrfest & World Cup Freestyle in January, is a paean to Ullr, Norse God of Snow. From Denver, 70 miles west on I-70.

ALLAIRE TIMBERS INN

9511 Hwy. 9   PO Box 4653   Breckenridge, CO 80424   (303) 453-7530
Jack & Kathy Gumph, Resident Owners   *(800) 624-4904*

LOCATION	South Main St. (Hwy. 9), on west side
OPEN	All Year
DESCRIPTION	1991 Log & Stone Rustic country furnishings
NO. OF ROOMS	10 w/private baths (including 2 suites)
RATES	Seasonal Rates: $85-195 Reservation/cancellation policy
CREDIT CARDS	MasterCard, Visa
BREAKFAST	Summer/Continental plus Winter/Full Served in dining room
AMENITIES	Spa on main deck, saunas & fireplaces in suites, decks on all rooms, robes, radios in rooms, phone & fireplace in common room, complimentary afternoon beverages, meeting facilities, limited handicapped access, ski, golf & bicycle storage
RESTRICTIONS	No smoking. No pets (resident dogs). Children over 12
RSO	Breckenridge Resort Chamber Service
MEMBER	B&B Innkeepers of Colorado Professional Assn. of Innkeepers International Summit County B&B Assn.

COTTEN HOUSE

102 S. French St.   PO Box 387   Breckenridge, CO 80424
Peter & Georgette Contos, Resident Owners   *(303) 453-5509*

LOCATION	2 blocks east of Main St. in Historic District
OPEN	All Year
DESCRIPTION	1886 Victorian Eclectic furnishings National Historic Register
NO. OF ROOMS	1 w/private bath 2 w/shared bath
RATES	Summer/PB/$50 SB/$40-45 Winter/PB/$100 SB/$70-80 Reservation/cancellation policy
CREDIT CARDS	No
BREAKFAST	Full, served in dining room
AMENITIES	Cable TV in 1 room, TV/VCR/stereo, phone, games, & books in common room, complimentary afternoon refreshments, ski lockers, bicycle storage, ski shuttle at front door. Inquire about meeting facilities
RESTRICTIONS	No smoking. No pets (resident parrot)
RSO	B&B Rocky Mountains
MEMBER	B&B Innkeepers of Colorado Summit County B&B Assn.

FIRESIDE INN

114 N. French St.   PO Box 2252   Breckenridge, CO 80424
Mary & Mike Keeling, Resident Owners   (303) 453-6456

LOCATION	Corner of French & Wellington Sts., 2 blocks from Main St. in center of Historic District
OPEN	All Year. B&B in summer only
DESCRIPTION	1879 Victorian w/1971 addition Victorian furnishings National Historic Register
NO. OF ROOMS	4 w/private baths 5 w/shared baths
RATES	PB/$40-125 SB/$13-30 Reservation/cancellation policy
CREDIT CARDS	MasterCard, Visa
BREAKFAST	Continental, served in dining room Full available at small additional charge
AMENITIES	Hot tub, all rooms w/cable TV/HBO, fireplace in parlor, guest phones, ski workbench & storage, bicycle storage, on free ski shuttle stop
RESTRICTIONS	No smoking. No pets. Inquire about children
REVIEWED	*The Colorado Guide* *Fodor's Colorado* *Recommended Country Inns of the Rocky Mountain Region*
RSO	Breckenridge Resort Chamber
MEMBER	Summit County B&B Assn.

HUMMINGBIRD HOUSE
BED & BREAKFAST

217 Hummingbird Dr.   PO Box 1354   Breckenridge, CO 80424
Bob & Betty Flint, Resident Owners   (303) 453-6957   (800) 723-8415

LOCATION	1-1/2 mi. from base of Peak 9 ski area
OPEN	All Year
DESCRIPTION	1981 2-Story Frame Traditional furnishings
NO. OF ROOMS	2 w/private baths 1 w/shared bath
RATES	PB/$65-75 SB/$50-55 Reservation/cancellation policy 2-night minimum during ski season
CREDIT CARDS	No
BREAKFAST	Full, served in dining room
AMENITIES	Outdoor jacuzzi, separate living area includes living room, TV/stereo, wet bar, microwave/refrigerator, wood burning stove, private entrance
RESTRICTIONS	Smoking limited. No pets (resident cat)
RSO	B&B Rocky Mountains

ONE WELLINGTON SQUARE

1 Wellington Sq.   PO Box 2967   Breckenridge, CO 80424
Jan & Mike Marshall, Resident Owners   (303) 453-6196

LOCATION	Center of Historic District
OPEN	All Year
DESCRIPTION	1978 Victorian Eclectic furnishings
NO. OF ROOMS	2 w/shared baths
RATES	$30-60 Reservation/cancellation policy 3-night minimum during ski season
CREDIT CARDS	No
BREAKFAST	Summer/Continental Winter/Full Served in dining room
AMENITIES	TV/radio in rooms, off-street parking, on ski shuttle route
RESTRICTIONS	No smoking. No pets. No small children
RSO	B&B Rocky Mountains
MEMBER	Summit County B&B Assn.

Ridge Street Inn Bed & Breakfast

212 N. Ridge St.   PO Box 2854   Breckenridge, CO 80424
Carol Brownson, Resident Owner   (303) 453-4680

LOCATION	Center of Historic District, 1 block east of Main St.
OPEN	All Year
DESCRIPTION	1890 Victorian Antique furnishings
NO. OF ROOMS	2 w/private baths 2 w/shared baths Dorm w/shared baths
RATES	Summer/PB/$45 SB/$40 Winter/PB/$88-95 SB/$78-85 Inquire about dorms Reservation/cancellation policy 2-night minimum in summer, 5-nights in winter
CREDIT CARDS	MasterCard, Visa
BREAKFAST	Full, served in commons area
AMENITIES	Aprés ski in winter, TV/phone available, limited use of kitchen, off-street parking
RESTRICTIONS	No smoking. No pets (resident dog & cat)
REVIEWED	*The Colorado Guide* *Fodor's B&B Guide*
RSO	B&B Rocky Mountains Breckenridge Resort Chamber

Swiss Inn Bed & Breakfast

205 S. French St.   PO Box 556   Breckenridge, CO 80424   (303) 453-6489
Sandy & Dan Gnos, Resident Owners   FAX: (303) 453-4915

LOCATION	Center of Breckenridge, 2 blocks from Main St.
OPEN	All Year
DESCRIPTION	1910 Victorian European furnishings National Historic Register
NO. OF ROOMS	2 w/private baths 2 w/shared baths 2 Dorms w/shared baths
RATES	Summer/PB/$50 SB/$45 Winter/PB/$78-100 SB/$65-85 Dorms/$15-30
CREDIT CARDS	For check guarantee only
BREAKFAST	Summer/Continental plus Winter/Full Served in dining room
AMENITIES	Hot tub, TV in rooms, 2 common areas w/fireplaces & cable TV/phone, complimentary afternoon refreshments
RESTRICTIONS	No smoking. No pets. No children

The Walker House

103 S. French St.   PO Box 509   Breckenridge, CO 80424
Pete & Georgette Contos, Managers   (800) 733-8415

LOCATION	In Historic District, 2 blocks from Main St.
OPEN	Nov. 1-May 15
DESCRIPTION	1875 Log Victorian Original Victorian furnishings
NO. OF ROOMS	1 w/private bath 1 w/shared bath

60

RATES	PB/$109 SB/$87
	Reservation/cancellation policy
	2-night minimum
CREDIT CARDS	For deposit only: American Express, Diner's Club, Discover, MasterCard, Visa
BREAKFAST	Continental plus, served in dining room or kitchen
AMENITIES	Robes, radio in rooms, complimentary refreshments, free pass for use of hot tub/sauna
RESTRICTIONS	None. Resident cat
REVIEWED	*Feather Beds & Flapjacks*
RSO	B&B Rocky Mountains
MEMBER	Summit County B&B Assn.

WILLIAMS HOUSE BED & BREAKFAST

303 N. Main St.   PO Box 2454   Breckenridge, CO 80424   (303) 453-2975
Diane Jaynes & Fred Kinat, Resident Owners

LOCATION	Center of town, west side of Main St.
OPEN	All Year
DESCRIPTION	1885 Victorian "Boomtown", Restored 1987 Antique furnishings
NO. OF ROOMS	4 w/private baths
RATES	Summer/$55-65 Winter/$89-137 Reservation/cancellation policy 3-night minimum during ski season
CREDIT CARDS	American Express
BREAKFAST	Full, served in dining area
AMENITIES	Sunroom & parlor w/radio/TV/VCR/stereo & fireplaces, complimentary afternoon refreshments, private off-street parking
RESTRICTIONS	No smoking. No pets (resident dog). No children
REVIEWED	*The Colorado Guide*
MEMBER	B&B Innkeepers of Colorado

Woodside B&B

157 Independence Circle   PO Box 2829   Breckenridge, CO 80424
Linda A. Otto & Jeff Blum, Resident Owners   (303) 453-7778

LOCATION	On Peak 7, 4 mi. north of town
OPEN	All Year (Closed during May)
DESCRIPTION	1980 Contemporary Mt. Chalet Oriental & southwestern furnishings
NO. OF ROOMS	3 w/private baths
RATES	$50-95 Reservation/cancellation policy
CREDIT CARDS	No
BREAKFAST	Full gourmet, served in dining room, or on sundeck
AMENITIES	Robes, TV/radio in rooms, wood-burning stove in common area, complimentary afternoon refreshments
RESTRICTIONS	No smoking. No pets. No children
RSO	Breckenridge Resort Chamber Central Reservations

BROOMFIELD

A growing city halfway between Denver & Boulder via Hwy. 36.

BROOMFIELD GUEST HOUSE

9009 W. Jeffco Airport Ave.   Broomfield, CO 80021   (303) 469-3900
Shirley Lindow, Resident Manager   FAX: (303) 438-1457

LOCATION	1/4 mi. east of Jeffco Ariport
OPEN	All Year
DESCRIPTION	1988 Contemporary Country Contemporary furnishings
NO. OF ROOMS	16 w/private baths
RATES	$90-100 Reservation/cancellation policy
CREDIT CARDS	American Express, Diner's Club, MasterCard, Visa
BREAKFAST	Continental plus, served in dining room
AMENITIES	Greenhouse w/jacuzzi, robes, TV/radio/phones/fireplaces in rooms, complimentary beverages, laundry room, private parking, meeting facilities, handicapped access
RESTRICTIONS	No pets

BUENA VISTA

A ranching and agricultural community 117 miles southwest of Denver on Hwy. 285. This beautiful area offers up the soaring Sawatch Range and Collegiate Range, whitewater rafting on the Arkansas River, the gem fields of Mt. Antero and Ruby Mountain, a natural hot springs resort, and the lofty mountain passes of Cottonwood, Tin Cup and Monarch for hiking and skiing.

THE ADOBE INN

303 N. Highway 24   PO Box 1560   Buena Vista, CO 81211
Paul & Marjorie Knox, Resident Owners   (719) 395-6340

LOCATION	Hwy. 24 at Stirling Ave., 2 blocks north of stoplight
OPEN	All Year
DESCRIPTION	1982 Southwestern Adobe Hacienda w/gourmet Mexican Restaurant Southwestern furnishings
NO. OF ROOMS	5 w/private baths
RATES	$44-69 Reservation/cancellation policy
CREDIT CARDS	MasterCard, Visa
BREAKFAST	Full, served in solarium
AMENITIES	Jacuzzi, Mexican tiled solarium w/fireplace, piano & library, one guest room w/adobe fireplace, cable TV in rooms, complimentary refreshments
RESTRICTIONS	No smoking. No pets
REVIEWED	*America's Wonderful Little Hotels & Inns* *The Colorado B&B Guide* *The Colorado Guide* *Recommended Country Inns of the Rocky Mountain Region*
MEMBER	B&B Innkeepers of Colorado
RATED	AAA 3 Diamonds

BLUE SKY INN

719 Arizona St.   Buena Vista, CO 81211   (719) 395-8862
Hazel Davis, Resident Owner

LOCATION	East of downtown Buena Vista, on Arkansas River
OPEN	All Year
DESCRIPTION	Contemporary Inn On 25 riverfront acres 2 buildings w/decks & terraces Antique & oriental rug furnishings
NO. OF ROOMS	6 w/private baths
RATES	$59.50-79.50
CREDIT CARDS	American Express, Master Card, Visa
BREAKFAST	Full, served in garden room overlooking river
AMENITIES	Complimentary afternoon tea & cookies, indoor greenhouse w/wood stove, living/recreation areas w/4 riverock fireplaces, library, guest kitchens, fishing in Arkansas River
RESTRICTIONS	No smoking. No pets
REVIEWED	*The Colorado Guide*
RSO	B&B Rocky Mountains

BLUEBIRD RIDGE BED & BREAKFAST

28483 County Road 340   Buena Vista, CO 81211   (719) 395-2336
Grace Huff, Resident Owner

LOCATION	4 mi. west of Buena Vista, in the foothills of Mt. Yale
OPEN	June-October 1
DESCRIPTION	1975 Log Chalet Early American furnishings
NO. OF ROOMS	2 w/private baths
RATES	$55
CREDIT CARDS	No
BREAKFAST	Full, served in dining room
AMENITIES	Complimentary refreshments on arrival, 1 room w/fireplace, small meeting facilities, handicapped access
RESTRICTIONS	No smoking. No pets

THE POTTER'S HOUSE BED & BREAKFAST

28490 Chaffee County Rd. 313   PO Box 1842   Buena Vista, CO 81211
Veryl Y. Rember, Resident Owner   (719) 395-6458

LOCATION	1 mi. south of town
OPEN	May 20-Oct. 15
DESCRIPTION	1986 Adobe Guesthouse Antique furnishings
NO. OF ROOMS	1 w/private bath 2 w/shared baths

RATES	PB/$70-80 SB/$60-70
	Reservation/cancellation policy
	5-day minimum stay
CREDIT CARDS	MasterCard, Visa
BREAKFAST	Full, served in dining room or garden patios
	Sack lunches available
AMENITIES	Fireplace in 1 room, complimentary refreshments
RESTRICTIONS	No smoking. No pets (resident dog). Children under 12

STREAMSIDE BED & BREAKFAST

18820 County Rd. 162   Nathrop, CO 81236   (719) 395-2553
Denny & Kathy Claveau, Resident Owners

LOCATION	In Chalk Creek Canyon on Chalk Creek, 7.5 mi. south of Buena Vista on Hwy. 285, 8 mi. west on County Rd. 162, 1 mi. from the Coronado Trail
OPEN	All Year
DESCRIPTION	1973 Rustic
	Country & traditional furnishings
NO. OF ROOMS	3 w/private baths
RATES	Sgl/$45 Dbl/$49
	Reservation/cancellation policy
	2-night minimum on holiday weekends
CREDIT CARDS	No
BREAKFAST	Full, served in dining area
AMENITIES	Picnic table, fire pit, lounge chairs on streamside
RESTRICTIONS	No smoking. No pets. Please inquire about children

TROUT CITY INN

PO Box 431   Buena Vista, CO 81211   *Summer: (719) 395-8433*
Juel & Irene Kjeldsen, Resident Owners   *Off season: (719) 495-0348*

LOCATION	On Trout Creek Pass, 5 mi. east of Buena Vista on Hwys. 285 & 24, and McGee Gulch Rd.
OPEN	June-October 1
DESCRIPTION	Exact replica of historic 1880 Victorian country railway depot McGee's Station & railroad cars Antique furnishings Arabian horse breeding & training ranch
NO. OF ROOMS	4 w/private baths 2 rms. in Depot; 1 in Private Pullman Car; 1 in Caboose
RATES	$35-40 Inquire about special group rates Reservation/cancellation policy
CREDIT CARDS	MasterCard, Visa
BREAKFAST	Full buffet, served in railroad depot ticket office Catered group buffet available
AMENITIES	Complimentary afternoon get acquainted party, sun deck, game room, VCR library, trout stream, gold prospecting, Victorian livery museum & mercantile store, special Weekend Getaway packages, small meeting facilities
RESTRICTIONS	No smoking. No pets (resident critters: dogs, cat, ducks, geese, horses & wildlife). Inquire about children
REVIEWED	*The Colorado Guide* *Great Affordable B&B Getaways* *Recommended Country Inns of the Rocky Mountain Region*
MEMBER	B&B Innkeepers of Colorado

BUFFALO CREEK

A beautiful wooded area in the Pike National Forest, 45 miles southwest of Denver and just south of Conifer via Hwy. 285 and SR 67.

THE BLUE JAY INN

PO Box 186   18051 Hwy. 126   Buffalo Creek, CO 80425   (303) 835-5945
Winter: 2100 E. Eastman Ave., Englewood, CO 80110   (303) 789-3115
Katherine Davis Ramus, Resident Owner

LOCATION	On Jefferson County Hwy., across from Forest Service Station
OPEN	June 15-Labor Day Weekend
DESCRIPTION	1880 English Inn Antique furnishings National Historic Register
NO. OF ROOMS	7 w/2 shared baths
RATES	$40-70 Reservation/cancellation policy
CREDIT CARDS	No
BREAKFAST	Full, served in dining room Lunch, dinner & catered receptions available
AMENITIES	Phone available, fireplaces in lobby & living room, porch, gift & book shop on premises, meeting/reception facilities
RESTRICTIONS	No smoking. No pets

CARBONDALE

A relatively new and young community, 30 miles northwest of Aspen on Hwy. 82. The Summer Mountain Fair in July is a major event.

AMBIANCE INN

66 N. Second St. Carbondale, CO 81623 (303) 963-3597
Robert & Norma Morris, Resident Owners

LOCATION	Center of Carbondale, 1/2 block east of Main St.
OPEN	All Year
DESCRIPTION	1975 Contemporary Manor House
NO. OF ROOMS	4 w/private baths
RATES	$60-100 Reservation/cancellation policy
CREDIT CARDS	MasterCard, Visa
BREAKFAST	Full, served in dining room Dinner by prior arrangement, extra charge
AMENITIES	Hot tub/sauna, robes, radios in rooms, TV/phones available, smoking area, complimentary refreshments
RESTRICTIONS	Smoking limited. No pets
REVIEWED	*The Colorado B&B Guide*
RSO	B&B Rocky Mountains Glenwood Springs Chamber Resort Assn.
MEMBER	B&B Innkeepers of Colorado

Aspen Valley Bed & Breakfast

16613 Hwy. 82   Carbondale, CO 81623
Chuck & Judy Nielsen, Resident Owners

(303) 963-2628
(800) 882-3193

LOCATION	6 mi. east of Carbondale
OPEN	All Year
DESCRIPTION	1974 Frame Ranch & Cabins Antique & contemporary furnishings
NO. OF ROOMS	3 w/private baths 3 w/shared bath
RATES	PB/$40-75 SB/$45-55 Reservation/cancellation policy 2-night minimum on weekends
CREDIT CARDS	American Express, MasterCard, Visa
BREAKFAST	Full, served in dining room Dinner, lunch & special meals available
AMENITIES	Complimentary refreshments, TV/radio in rooms, phone & fireplace in common room. Owners specialize in fly fishing & fly-tying lessons, 35mm photography workshops, fishing in private ponds and Roaring Fork River
RESTRICTIONS	Limited smoking. No pets (resident dogs). Inquire about children

THE BIGGERSTAFF HOUSE

0318 Lions Ridge Rd.   Carbondale, CO 81623   (303) 963-3605
Jack & Jane E. Van Horn, Resident Owners

LOCATION	3 1/2 mi. past Carbondale exit, near intersection of Hwy. 82 & Road 100
OPEN	All Year
DESCRIPTION	1982 Bavarian-style farmhouse Antique furnishings
NO. OF ROOMS	4 w/shared baths
RATES	Sgl/$40 Dbl/$50 Reservation/cancellation policy
CREDIT CARDS	MasterCard, Visa
BREAKFAST	Full, served in dining room
AMENITIES	Robes, guest lounge w/TV, books, & games, complimentary refreshments, 2 rooms w/balconies
RESTRICTIONS	No smoking. No pets. No children
REVIEWED	*Christian B&B Directory* *Recommended Country Inns of the Rocky Mountain Region*
RSO	B&B Rocky Mountains
MEMBER	B&B Innkeepers of Colorado

CASCADE
(COLORADO SPRINGS)

A small residential mountain town, in the Ute Pass area, west of Colorado Springs via Hwy. 24. Distances vary, depending on where you are. From the Statue of General Palmer and his horse in downtown Colorado Springs, it is said to be 9.9 miles (unless the horse is moved in the near future).

EASTHOLME BED & BREAKFAST

PO Box 98 4445 Haggerman   Cascade, CO 80809   (719) 684-9901/2145
Harland & Joan Jacobson, Resident Owners

LOCATION	On corner of Topeka & Haggerman, 1 mi. north of Pikes Peak Hwy., in Pike National Forest
OPEN	All Year
DESCRIPTION	1885 Restored Victorian Antique furnishings Designated Ute Pass Landmark
NO. OF ROOMS	4 w/private baths 2 w/shared bath 2 cabins w/private baths (1 w/fireplace)
RATES	$39-64 Inquire about group rates Reservation/cancellation policy
CREDIT CARDS	No
BREAKFAST	Full, served in dining area
AMENITIES	40 ft. porch & balcony, Guest Parlor w/cable TV/VCR, piano & fireplace, Guest Kitchen, library
RESTRICTIONS	No smoking. No pets (resident dog). Children over 10
AWARDS	Colorado Excellence in Preservation Award, Colorado Preservation, Inc.
RSO	B&B Rocky Mountains
MEMBER	B&B Innkeepers of Colorado

CEDAREDGE

Known as the southern gateway to Grand Mesa, 60 miles southwest of Grand Junction, via Delta on Hwys. 92 & Scenic 65. The Apple Festival in October is a major event.

CEDARS' EDGE LLAMAS BED & BREAKFAST

2169 Highway 65   Cedaredge, CO 81413   (303) 856-6836
Ray & Gail Record, Resident Owners

LOCATION	5 mi north of Cedaredge on Hwy. 65
OPEN	All Year
DESCRIPTION	1982 Contemporary Cedar, Passive Solar Country furnishings Working llama ranch
NO. OF ROOMS	3 w/private baths 1 suite w/private bath & bathtub for two
RATES	$35-85 Reservation/cancellation policy
CREDIT CARDS	No
BREAKFAST	Full, served in sunroom, guestrooms or on decks Gourmet llama picnics & dayhikes available
AMENITIES	Llamas, llamas, llamas. Learn to halter, lead, groom a llama & everything else. Also, private decks, TV/radio, small meeting facilities
RESTRICTIONS	No smoking. No pets
REVIEWED	*B&B U.S.A.* *The Colorado Guide*
RSO	B&B Rocky Mountains
MEMBER	B&B Innkeepers of Colorado

CENTRAL CITY

Victorian mining town and National Historic District, 30 miles northwest of Denver via I-70 and Idaho Springs exit, 1 mile west of Black Hawk on Hwy. 279. Known for its Summer Opera and Jazz Festival, and narrow gauge railroad. And now there's small stakes gambling.

CENTRAL CITY MANOR, INC., A VICTORIAN GUESTHOUSE

---

325 Spring St.   Central City, CO 80427   *(303) 582-5038*
Mailing address: 1598 Hyland Dr.   Evergreen, CO 80439
Deborah Pranke, Resident Owner   *(800) 426-1284*

LOCATION	Corner of Spring & Roworth Sts., 1 block south of gaming district, just past railroad station
OPEN	All Year
DESCRIPTION	1876 Victorian Victorian furnishings
NO. OF ROOMS	1 w/private bath 3 w/shared baths
RATES	PB/$125 SB/$65 Reservation/cancellation policy
CREDIT CARDS	MasterCard, Visa
BREAKFAST	Continental, served in lobby Complimentary $5.00 food certificates for Mainstreet Gaming House in Black Hawk
AMENITIES	Phone in rooms, complimentary amenity basket, free parking
RESTRICTIONS	No smoking. No pets
RSO	Central Reservations (303) 278-7859

THE VICTORIAN INN

205 W. High St.   PO Box 31   Central City, CO 80427   (303) 582-0516
Tad Entrup, Resident Owner

LOCATION	1/2 block northwest of Teller House & Gaming District
OPEN	All Year
DESCRIPTION	1872 Victorian Victorian furnishings National Historic Register
NO. OF ROOMS	3 w/private baths 1 w/shared bath
RATES	Call for current rates Reservation/cancellation policy
CREDIT CARDS	American Express, MasterCard, Visa
BREAKFAST	Continental, served in dining room
AMENITIES	Robes, TV/radio in rooms, complimentary refreshments & game tokens, meeting facilities
RESTRICTIONS	Inquire about pets (resident dog). No children
RSO	Central Reservations (303) 278-7859

WINFIELD SCOTT GUESTQUARTERS BED & BREAKFAST

Suites PO Box 369   210 Hooper St.   Central City, CO 80427
(303) 582-3433   FAX: (303) 582-3434
Patty & Scott Webb, Resident Owners

LOCATION	On hill above parking lots, near gaming district
OPEN	All Year
DESCRIPTION	1991 Victorian Chalet Country & southwestern furnishings
NO. OF ROOMS	1 1-bedroom suite, w/private bath & kitchen 1 2-bedroom suite, w/private bath & kitchen
RATES	$79-149 Reservation/cancellation policy
CREDIT CARDS	MasterCard, Visa
BREAKFAST	Continental plus, served in suites
AMENITIES	TV/VCR, radio, phone in suites, fireplace in 2-bedroom suite, complimentary refreshments, outdoor grill & picnic tables
RESTRICTIONS	No smoking. No pets (resident dog)
RSO	Central Reservations (303) 278-7859

CHIPITA PARK
(COLORADO SPRINGS)

A mountain town in the beautiful Ute Pass area, 18 miles west of Colorado Springs via Hwy. 24. Near the entrance to Pikes Peak Highway.

TOP OF TIMPA

5620 Timpa Rd.   Chipita Park, CO 80809   *(719) 684-2296*
Mailing address: PO Box 425   Cascade, CO 80809   *(800) 524-9819*
Dick & Elizabeth Dolbee, Resident Owners

LOCATION	Between Cascade & Green Mountain Falls. Hwy. 24 west to Pikes Peak/Cascade Exit, northwest on Chipita Park Rd., then south on Timpa Rd. all the way to the top
OPEN	All Year
DESCRIPTION	1957 Mountain Compound Eclectic furnishings
NO. OF ROOMS	2 suites w/private baths 2 guesthouses w/private baths
RATES	$60-70 Reservation/cancellation policy
CREDIT CARDS	MasterCard, Visa
BREAKFAST	Full, continental plus or continental served in dining room or guestrooms
AMENITIES	8-person hot tub/sauna, robes, TV/radio/phones, refrigerators in rooms, fireplace in 1 room, complimentary evening snacks, laundry & meeting facilities, outdoor areas fully illuminated, stable/corral can accommodate 2 horses
RESTRICTIONS	No smoking. No pets

CLARK

Former gold mining boom area, 25 miles north of Steamboat Springs at Hahn's Peak. Near Steamboat Lake and Hahn's Peak Lake.

THE INN AT STEAMBOAT LAKE

61027 County Rd. 129   Hahn's Peak, CO   (303) 879-3906
Mailing address: PO Box 839   Clark, CO 80428   (800) 934-7829
Tim Leonard & John Leonard, Resident Owners

LOCATION	On Steamboat Lake, 25 mi. north of Steamboat Springs at Hahn's Peak, in Routt National Forest
OPEN	All Year
DESCRIPTION	2-Story Log Lodge w/Restaurant
NO. OF ROOMS	8 w/private baths
RATES	$69-75
CREDIT CARDS	Discover, MasterCard, Visa
BREAKFAST	Continental plus, served in dining room
AMENITIES	Hot tub, guest lounge w/satellite TV, wood-burning stove, complimentary refreshments, handicapped access, meeting/conference facilities
RESTRICTIONS	None
RSO	B&B Rocky Mountains
MEMBER	Colorado Campground and CabinResort Assn.

COALMONT

A small rural town 45 miles east of Steamboat Springs, half-way between Walden and Rabbit Ears Pass at Hwy. 4 & 14.

SHAMROCK RANCH

4363 Rd. 11   Coalmont, CO 80430   Summer: (303) 723-8413
Bruce & Cindy Wilson, Resident Owners   Winter: (303) 986-3616

LOCATION	20 mi. east of U.S. 40 & Hwy. 14, east side of Rabbit Ears Pass
OPEN	May 22-October 4
DESCRIPTION	1934 Log Homestead Western antique furnishings
NO. OF ROOMS	7 w/5 shared baths
RATES	$90-160 Reservation/cancellation policy
CREDIT CARDS	No
BREAKFAST	Full, served in dining area or guestrooms Gourmet dinners included in rate Lunch & special meals available on request
AMENITIES	Complimentary special hour w/hors d'oeurves, trout fishing on property, horseback riding
RESTRICTIONS	Smoking limited. No pets (resident critters: dogs, chickens, rabbit, lambs, pigs, horses)
RSO	B&B Rocky Mountains

COLORADO SPRINGS

Purple Mountain Majesties start here. Nestled at the foot of Pikes Peak, the state's second largest city was the inspiration for *America the Beautiful*. It's now a major military, amateur sports, industrial and tourist center, 65 miles south of Denver on I-25.

BLACK FOREST BED & BREAKFAST

11170 Black Forest Rd. Colorado Springs, CO 80908 (719) 495-4208
Robert & Susan Putnam, Resident Owners

LOCATION	I-25 Exit 149, 6 mi. east on Woodmen Rd., 3-1/2 mi. north on Black Forest Rd.
OPEN	All Year
DESCRIPTION	1984 Dutch Colonial log On 20 forested acres Rustic furnishings
NO. OF ROOMS	Main House: 2 w/private baths & kitchenettes Guesthouse: 1 w/private bath, full kitchen, laundry facilities
RATES	$65-75 Reservation/cancellation policy
CREDIT CARDS	MasterCard, Visa
BREAKFAST	Continental plus, served in guest rooms
AMENITIES	Fireplaces & TV/radio/phone in rooms, complimentary refreshments
RESTRICTIONS	No smoking. No pets (resident critters: dog, cat, chickens, pheasants)
RSO	B&B Rocky Mountains
MEMBER	B&B Innkeepers of Colorado

GRIFFIN'S HOSPITALITY HOUSE

4222 W. Chestnut St. Colorado Springs, CO 80907 (719) 599-3035
John & Diane Griffin, Resident Owners

Please inquire about rates and other information

HEARTHSTONE INN

506 N. Cascade   Colorado Springs, CO 80903   (719) 473-4413
Ruth Williams & Dot Williams, Owners

LOCATION	4 blocks north of downtown, 3 blocks south of Colorado College
OPEN	All Year
DESCRIPTION	1885 3-Story Queen Anne Victorian, 2 connected buildings Antique furnishings National Historic Register
NO. OF ROOMS	23 w/private baths 2 w/shared bath
RATES	$78-120 Reservation/cancellation policy
CREDIT CARDS	American Express, MasterCard, Visa
BREAKFAST	Full gourmet, served in dining room
AMENITIES	Complimentary refreshments, radio in rooms, 3 rooms w/wood burning fireplaces, meeting facilities and special meals for groups up to 48
RESTRICTIONS	No smoking. No pets.
REVIEWED	America's Wonderful Little Hotels & Inns The Colorado B&B Guide The Colorado Guide Country Inns & Backroads Country Inns & Bed & Breakfast Frommer's Denver, Boulder, & Colorado Springs The Old-House Lover's Guide to Inns and Bed & Breakfast Guest Houses Recommended Country Inns of the Rocky Mountain Region
MEMBER	Distinctive Inns of Colorado Colorado Hotel and Motel Assn. Historic Hotels of the Rocky Mountain West Independent Innkeepers Assn.
RATED	AAA 3 Diamonds Mobil 3 Stars

Holden House 1902 Bed & Breakfast Inn

1102 W. Pikes Peak Ave.   Colorado Springs, CO 80904   (719) 471-3980
Sallie & Welling Clark, Resident Owners

LOCATION	1 mi. west of downtown Colorado Springs, near Old Colorado City Historic District, Colorado Ave. to 11th St. & Pikes Peak
OPEN	All Year
DESCRIPTION	1902 Colonial Revival Victorian and & 1906 Carriage House Traditional & Antique furnishings
NO. OF ROOMS	2 w/private baths 3 suites w/fireplaces, sitting area & private baths
RATES	$57-85 Reservation/cancellation policy Inquire about minimum stays during holidays & special events
CREDIT CARDS	American Express, Discover, MasterCard, Visa
BREAKFAST	Full gourmet, served in dining room or on veranda
AMENITIES	Complimentary refreshments, tubs for two in 2 suites, sparkling water in rooms, turndown service, TV in parlor, air conditioning in summer, daily maid service
RESTRICTIONS	No smoking. No pets (resident cat). No children
AWARDS	1991 Top 50 Inns in America, *Inn Times*
REVIEWED	*America's Wonderful Little Hotels & Inns* *Best Places to Stay in the West* *Colorado B&B Guide* *The Colorado Guide* *Recommended Country Inns of the Rocky Mountain Region*
RSO	B&B Rocky Mountains Colorado Hotel & Lodging Assn.
MEMBER	B&B Innkeepers of Colorado Professional Assn. of Innkeepers International
RATED	AAA 3 Diamonds Mobil 2 Stars

THE PAINTED LADY
BED & BREAKFAST INN

1318 W. Colorado Ave.   Colorado Springs, CO 80904   (719) 473-3165
Kenneth & Stacey Kale, Resident Owners

LOCATION	4 blocks east of Old Colorado City & Colorado Ave., between 13th & 14th Sts.
OPEN	All Year
DESCRIPTION	1894 3-Story Victorian Country & antique furnishings
NO. OF ROOMS	2 w/private baths 2 w/shared bath 1 suite w/private bath
RATES	Rooms/PB/$60-80 SB/$45 Suite/$125 Inquire about minimum stay during holidays
CREDIT CARDS	MasterCard, Visa
BREAKFAST	Full, served in dining room or on veranda
AMENITIES	Complimentary evening refreshments, off-street parking, small meeting facilities
RESTRICTIONS	No smoking. No pets. No children

TUDOR MANOR

1332 N. Cascade Ave.   Colorado Springs, CO 80903   (719) 630-3433
Marlene & Biff Hallenbeck, Resident Owners   (800) 733-8415

LOCATION   In Historic Dictrict, 2 blocks north of Colorado college, I-25
                  Uintah Exit east to Cascade

OPEN   All Year

DESCRIPTION   1929 2-Story English Tudor
                  Original period furnishings

NO. OF ROOMS   4 w/shared or adjoining baths

RATES $59-69
                  Reservation/cancellation policy
                  2-night minimum stay or $10 added to rate

CREDIT CARDS   No

BREAKFAST   Full gourmet, served in formal dining room

AMENITIES   TV/radio in rooms, 1 room w/sunporch & patio,
                  complimentary evening refreshments, outdoor grill, library

RESTRICTIONS   No smoking. No pets. Children over 10

AWARDS   Best B&B Homestay Award, B&B Rocky Mountains

REVIEWED   *Colorado B&B Guide*

RSO   B&B Rocky Mountains

Como

A partial ghost town of the 1870's railroad era, in the South Park Valley, 75 miles southwest of Denver, 25 miles northeast of Fairplay on Hwy. 285. A rare, historic roundhouse still stands there.

Como Depot

PO Box 648   Como, CO 80432   (719) 836-2594
Keith & Jo Hodges, Resident Owners

LOCATION	9 mi. north of Fairplay, 1/4 mi. west of Hwy. 285
OPEN	March-December
DESCRIPTION	1898 Restored Railroad Depot w/Restaurant Eclectic furnishings National Historic Register
NO. OF ROOMS	4 w/shared bath
RATES	$25.00
CREDIT CARDS	No
BREAKFAST	Full, served in dining room Other meals available in restaurant
AMENITIES	1 room w/fireplace, clawfoot tub in bathroom Restaurant open 8:00 a.m.-8:00 p.m.
RESTRICTIONS	No pets
REVIEWED	*The Colorado Guide*

CREEDE

A tiny, isolated historic mining town nestled in the Rio Grande National Forest, 70 miles west of Alamosa on Hwy. 149, between South Fork and Lake City. Known for its Opera House and Repertory Theater, and the Wheeler Geologic Natural Area.

CREEDE HOTEL

1892 Main Street   PO Box 284   Creede, CO 81130   (719) 658-2608
Cathy & Rich Ormsby, Resident Owner

LOCATION	Downtown Creede, next door to the Creede Repertory Theatre
OPEN	April-Oct.
DESCRIPTION	1892 2-Story Western Hotel
NO. OF ROOMS	4 w/private baths
RATES	$45-60 Reservation/cancellation policy
CREDIT CARDS	Discover, MasterCard, Visa
BREAKFAST	Full gourmet, served in dining room Lunch/dinner available in restaurant
AMENITIES	2 rooms open onto front balcony, facilities for weddings & meetings
RESTRICTIONS	No pets. No smoking. Inquire about children
REVIEWED	*The Colorado Guide*
MEMBER	B&B Innkeepers of Colorado

CRAIG

Here in the northwest corner of the state, 42 miles west of Steamboat Springs on Hwy. 40, is the jumping-off place for exploring the Yampa and Green River Canyons, and Brown's Park Scenic & Historic Area. Or check out "Marcia", David Moffat's historic 1906 luxury Pullman Car in City Park, the Moffat County Chariot Races in February, and the Greek Festival in March.

ROSS'S RIVER RANCH BED & BREAKFAST

5529 Hwy. 394   Craig, CO 81625   (303) 824-5955
Jim & Kathy Ross, Resident Owners

LOCATION	Southeast of Craig. From Hwy. 40: South on Ronney St. to 1st intersection. 5.5 mi. east on Hwy. 394 to Ross's Acres Lane on left
OPEN	All Year
DESCRIPTION	1979 2-story Southern Antebellum Antique furnishings 250 acre working sheep & horse ranch
NO. OF ROOMS	2 w/private bath 1 suite w/private bath & woodstove
RATES	$30-35 Reservation/cancellation policy
CREDIT CARDS	No
BREAKFAST	Full, served in dining room Dinner available by advance request
AMENITIES	Swimming in private riverfront, hot tub, wood stove in suite, TV available, hunting, fishing/hiking/x-country skiing/horseback riding on property
RESTRICTIONS	No smoking. Pets restricted (resident critters: dogs, cats, horses, sheep)

CREEDE

A tiny, isolated historic mining town nestled in the Rio Grande National Forest, 70 miles west of Alamosa on Hwy. 149, between South Fork and Lake City. Known for its Opera House and Repertory Theater, and the Wheeler Geologic Natural Area.

CREEDE HOTEL

1892 Main Street   PO Box 284   Creede, CO 81130   (719) 658-2608
Cathy & Rich Ormsby, Resident Owner

LOCATION	Downtown Creede, next door to the Creede Repertory Theatre
OPEN	April-Oct.
DESCRIPTION	1892 2-Story Western Hotel
NO. OF ROOMS	4 w/private baths
RATES	$45-60 Reservation/cancellation policy
CREDIT CARDS	Discover, MasterCard, Visa
BREAKFAST	Full gourmet, served in dining room Lunch/dinner available in restaurant
AMENITIES	2 rooms open onto front balcony, facilities for weddings & meetings
RESTRICTIONS	No pets. No smoking. Inquire about children
REVIEWED	*The Colorado Guide*
MEMBER	B&B Innkeepers of Colorado

CRESTED BUTTE

A charming, Victorian mining town and major ski and summer resort, 30 miles north of Gunnison on Hwy. 136. This is paradise for skiers of deep and steep powder and double-black diamonds. Check out the Rocky Mountain Biology Lab, one of the country's most distinguished field stations; the exciting Aerial Weekend in July; and the ultimate Fat Tire Bike Week and Pearl Pass Classic in September.

ALPINE LACE, INC. BED & BREAKFAST

PO Box 2183   726 Maroon   Crested Butte, CO 81224   (303) 349-9857
Loree Mulay & Ward Weisman, Resident Owners

LOCATION	Corner of Maroon & 8th Sts., 2 blocks from shuttle
OPEN	All Year
DESCRIPTION	1967 Swiss Chalet European & antique furnishings
NO. OF ROOMS	2 w/private baths 2 w/shared bath
RATES	PB/$70-75 SB/$55-60 Reservation/cancellation policy Inquire about minimum stay depending on season
CREDIT CARDS	MasterCard, Visa
BREAKFAST	Full, served in dining room
AMENITIES	Jacuzzi, robes in shared bath, TV in master room, portable phone available, complimentary refreshments, ski & bike storage, sunroom & deck
RESTRICTIONS	No smoking. No pets. No children
RSO	B&B Rocky Mountains Crested Butte Vacations
MEMBER	American B&B Assn. B&B Innkeepers of Colorado

THE CLAIM JUMPER

PO Box 704   704 Whiterock   Crested Butte, CO 81224   (303) 349-6471
Jerry & Robbie Bigelow, Resident Owners

LOCATION	Center of town, across from Town Park
OPEN	All Year
DESCRIPTION	1960 Log Antique furnishings, memorabilia
NO. OF ROOMS	2 w/private baths 4 share 2 baths
RATES	$50-85
CREDIT CARDS	No
BREAKFAST	Full gourmet, served in dining room
AMENITIES	Hot tub w/view of mountains, full sauna, antique game room, TV/VCR, wood burning stove
RESTRICTIONS	No smoking. No small children
REVIEWED	*The Colorado Guide*
RSO	B&B Rocky Mountains

THE CRESTED BEAUTY

PO Box 1204   329 Whiterock Ave.   Crested Butte, CO 81224
Dan McCord & Mike Gould, Resident Owners   (303) 349-1201

LOCATION	Southwest corner of 4th St. & Whiterock Ave.
OPEN	All Year
DESCRIPTION	1991 Victorian Eclectic furnishings
NO. OF ROOMS	6 w/3 shared baths
RATES	$55-95 Reservation/cancellation policy
CREDIT CARDS	MasterCard, Visa
BREAKFAST	Full, served in dining room Inquire about special meals Special diets accommodated
AMENITIES	Hot tub/sauna, complimentary beverages & aprés ski, fireplace & books in common room
RESTRICTIONS	No smoking. Pets limited (resident dog & cats). Children under 16

CRISTIANA GUESTHAUS
BED & BREAKFAST

PO Box 427   621 Maroon Ave.   Crested Butte, CO 81224
Rosie & Martin Catmur, Resident Owners   (303) 349-5326

LOCATION	1/2 block east of Hwy. 135, 1 block north of Elk Ave., 3 mi. south of ski area
OPEN	All Year
DESCRIPTION	1963 Alpine lodge Country furnishings

NO. OF ROOMS	21 w/private bath
RATES	Summer/$47-54 Winter/$50-82 Reservation/cancellation policy
CREDIT CARDS	American Express, Discover, MasterCard, Visa
BREAKFAST	Continental plus, served fireside in lounge
AMENITIES	Outdoor hot tub, sauna, TV, fireplace & books in lounge, complimentary beverages, ski & bicycle storage
RESTRICTIONS	Smoking limited. No pets (resident cat)
REVIEWED	*The Colorado Guide* *Fodor's Colorado*

THE GOTHIC INN

18 Gothic Ave.   PO Box 1488   Crested Butte, CO 81224   (303) 349-7215
Sonja Ruta, Resident Owner

LOCATION	Center of town, 2 blocks from the main street
OPEN	All Year
DESCRIPTION	1982 Contemporary Wood On 4 lots European style furnishings
NO. OF ROOMS	3 w/private baths 2 w/shared bath
RATES	$60-150 Reservation/cancellation policy 3-night minimum in winter
CREDIT CARDS	MasterCard, Visa
BREAKFAST	Full gourmet, served in dining room
AMENITIES	Hot tub, complimentary refreshments, 1 room w/private entry
RESTRICTIONS	No smoking. No pets. No children

Purple Mountain Lodge

PO Box 897   714 Gothic Ave.   Crested Butte, CO 81224
Sherron & Walter Green, Resident Owners   (303) 349-5888

LOCATION	Northeast end of town, near ski lifts
OPEN	All Year
DESCRIPTION	1927 Lodge
NO. OF ROOMS	3 w/private baths 2 w/shared bath
RATES	PB/$45-72 SB/$62
CREDIT CARDS	Diner's Club, Discover, MasterCard, Visa
BREAKFAST	Full, served in dining room
AMENITIES	Hot tub, sun room, cable TV & fireplace in living room, phone available
RESTRICTIONS	No smoking. No pets (resident dog). Inquire about children

THE TUDOR ROSE BED & BREAKFAST

PO Box 337   429 Whiterock   Crested Butte, CO 81224   (303) 349-6253
Sherri Deetz & Mike Nelson, Resident Owners

LOCATION	Center of Crested Butte in Historic District
OPEN	All Year
DESCRIPTION	1976 French Mansard Country furnishings
NO. OF ROOMS	5 w/2 shared bath
RATES	$55-75 Reservation/cancellation policy
CREDIT CARDS	MasterCard, Visa
BREAKFAST	Full, served in dining room
AMENITIES	Hot tub, 1 room w/wood burning stove, occasional complimentary refreshments
RESTRICTIONS	No smoking. Limited pets. Limited children
REVIEWED	*The Colorado B&B Guide*
MEMBER	B&B Innkeepers of Colorado

CRIPPLE CREEK

This historic mining area and summer tourist town 40 miles southwest of Colorado Springs via Hwy. 24 & 67 now has small stakes gambling to attract visitors. In the fall, the town is a prime destination for aspen-viewing.

HOTEL ST. NICHOLAS

PO Box 179   233 E. Eaton St.   Cripple Creek, CO 80813
(800) 352-5235   FAX: (719) 689-2338
Stephen Soares, Manager

LOCATION	2 blocks north of Bennett St., at 3rd & Eaton
OPEN	All Year
DESCRIPTION	1899 Victorian Victorian furnishings National Historic Register
NO. OF ROOMS	21 w/shared baths
RATES	$40-60 Reservation/cancellation policy
CREDIT CARDS	Discover, MasterCard, Visa
BREAKFAST	Continental, served in dining room
AMENITIES	Complimentary coffee, meeting facilities
RESTRICTIONS	None

OVER THE RAINBOW BED & BREAKFAST

PO Box 778   315 E. Eaton   Cripple Creek, CO 80813   (719) 689-3108
Karen Mulcahy, Resident Owner

LOCATION	2 blocks north of Historic District & Casinos
OPEN	All Year

DESCRIPTION	1890 Victorian
NO. OF ROOMS	3 w/shared bath
RATES	$40-50 Reservation/cancellation policy
CREDIT CARDS	MasterCard, Visa
BREAKFAST	Continental plus, served in dining room
RESTRICTIONS	No smoking. No pets (resident cats)

WILD BILL'S PUB, GAMING PARLOR, BED & BREAKFAST & RESTAURANT

220 E. Bennett Ave.   PO Box 928 or 180   Cripple Creek, CO 80813
Bill Large, Resident Owner   *(719) 689-2707/2482*

LOCATION	On town's main street, just west of Phoenix House
OPEN	All Year
DESCRIPTION	1896 Restored Victorian Antique & Victorian furnishings National Historic Register
NO. OF ROOMS	6 w/private baths 1 w/shared bath
RATES	$30-65 (Seasonal rates) Reservation/cancellation policy 2-night minimum during holidays
CREDIT CARDS	Discover, MasterCard, Visa
BREAKFAST	Continental plus, served in dining room Other meals available in pub & restaurant
AMENITIES	Complimentary refreshments, handicapped access to casino
RESTRICTIONS	Smoking limited. No pets

DEL NORTE

An agricultural area on the western edge of the San Luis Valley, 31 miles west of Alamosa on Hwys. 160 & 285. The Heritage Fair, Mountainmen Renegade Rendezvous, and Covered Wagon Days in August are major events.

WILD IRIS INN AT LA GARITA CREEK RANCH

38145 Rd. E-39   Del Norte, CO 81132   (719) 754-2533
Jeff & Liz Wilkin, Resident Managers

LOCATION	10 mi. north of Del Norte, off Hwy. 285
OPEN	Memorial Day-Thanksgiving (1 cabin available year round)
DESCRIPTION	1977 Contemporary Log & Cabins On 155 acres Rustic furnishings
NO. OF ROOMS	Lodge: 7 rooms share 5-1/2 baths 2 cabins w/private baths & fireplaces 1 2-room cabin w/2 private baths, full kitchen & wood-burning stove
RATES	PB/$56-66 SB/$38-48 Group rates available Reservation/cancellation policy
CREDIT CARDS	MasterCard, Visa
BREAKFAST	Continental plus, served in dining room Special meals available on request
AMENITIES	Swimming pool, hot tub/sauna, moss rock fireplace, satellite TV, piano & bar in lodge, tennis court, trout stream, meeting facilities, hot air ballooning, 12k Arch March in Oct.
RESTRICTIONS	Smoking limited. No pets (resident critters: dog, cats, ducks, geese)
RSO	Off the Beaten Path

Denver

Colorado's state capitol and largest city. The mile-high plains city surrounded by mountains is a major cosmopolitan, cultural, manufacturing and transportation center in the Rocky Mountain west.

Castle Marne

1572 Race St.   Denver, CO 80203   (303) 331-0621   FAX: (303) 331-0623
Jim & Diane Peiker, Resident Owners

LOCATION	16th Ave. & Race St., in downtown Denver
OPEN	All Year
DESCRIPTION	1889 Richardsonian/Romanesque Antique furnishings National Historic Register
NO. OF ROOMS	9 w/private baths
RATES	Sgl/$75-160 Dbl/$85-160 Reservation/cancellation policy
CREDIT CARDS	American Express, Diner's Club, Discover, MasterCard, Visa
BREAKFAST	Full gourmet, served in dining room Authentic Victorian teas & luncheons available
AMENITIES	Complimentary formal afternoon tea, some rooms w/jacuzzi tubs, robes, TV/radio/phones in rooms, meeting facilities
RESTRICTIONS	No smoking. No pets. No children
AWARDS	Stephen H. Hart Preservation Award, Colorado State Historical Society
REVIEWED	*Colorado B&B Guide* *Frommer's Denver, Boulder, & Colorado Springs*
MEMBER	Assn. of Historic Hotels of the West B&B Innkeepers of Colorado Colorado Hotel and Motel Assn. Distinctive Inns of Colorado Professional Assn. of Innkeepers International
RATED	AAA 3 Diamonds ABBA 4 Crowns Mobil 3 Stars

FRANKLIN HOUSE BED & BREAKFAST

1620 Franklin St.   Denver, CO 80218   (303) 331-9106
George & Sharon Bauer, Resident Owners

LOCATION	Residential neighborhood 16 blocks east of downtown, just north of Colfax
OPEN	All Year
DESCRIPTION	1890's Queen Anne Victorian Eclectic furnishings
NO. OF ROOMS	1 w/private bath 7 w/shared baths
RATES	PB/$35-40 SB/$20-30 Also weekly/monthly rates
CREDIT CARDS	Discover, MasterCard, Visa
BREAKFAST	Full, served in dining room
AMENITIES	Radio in rooms, central TV, BBQ, complimentary refreshments, off-street parking
RESTRICTIONS	No pets (resident cats)

THE HOLIDAY CHALET, A VICTORIAN HOTEL

1820 E. Colfax Ave.   Denver, CO 80218   (303) 321-9975   (800) 626-4497
Margot & Bob Hartmann, Resident Managers

LOCATION	15 blocks east of State Capitol, 2 blocks from Cheesman Park, 1/2 way between Broadway & Colorado Ave.
OPEN	All Year
DESCRIPTION	1896 3-Story Dutch Brownstone Victorian furnishings
NO. OF ROOMS	10 suites w/private baths & kitchens

100

RATES	$49-62.50
	Reservation/cancellation policy
CREDIT CARDS	American Express, Diner's Club, Discover, EnRoute, MasterCard, Visa
BREAKFAST	Continental, self-serve in suites
AMENITIES	TV/radio/phone in rooms, air-conditioning, fireplaces in 2 rooms, ice cream socials in summer, gas barbeque grills available
RESTRICTIONS	No smoking. Small pets only (resident dog)
REVIEWED	*The Colorado Guide*
RATED	AAA 3 Diamonds

MERRITT HOUSE
BED & BREAKFAST INN

941 E. 17th Ave. Denver, CO 80218 (303) 861-5230
Mary & Tom Touris, Resident Owners

LOCATION	Downtown, 8 blocks from State Capitol
OPEN	All Year
DESCRIPTION	1889 Victorian
	National Historic Register
NO. OF ROOMS	10 w/private baths
RATES	Rooms w/shower/$75-85
	Rooms w/whirlpool jacuzzi/$95-105
	Reservation/cancellation policy
CREDIT CARDS	American Express, MasterCard, Visa
BREAKFAST	Full, served in dining room
	Lunch available, dinners available by request
AMENITIES	TV/radio/phone in rooms
RESTRICTIONS	Smoking limited. No pets. Children over 12
AWARDS	Colorado Preservation Award 1988

THE QUEEN ANNE INN

2147 Tremont Place   Denver, CO 80205   (303) 296-6666   (800) 432-Inns
Ann & Charles Hillestad, Resident Owners   FAX: (303) 296-2151

LOCATION	Downtown Denver, in Clements Historic District
OPEN	All Year
DESCRIPTION	1879 2-Story Victorian Antique furnishings National Historic Register
NO. OF ROOMS	10 w/private baths
RATES	Sgl/PB/$54-114 Dbl/PB$64-124 Reservation/cancellation policy
CREDIT CARDS	American Express, Discover, EnRoute, Master Card, Visa
BREAKFAST	Continental plus, served in dining room, garden, or in bed by request
AMENITIES	Complimentary beverages, fruit, fresh flowers, air conditioning, chamber music, parlor, parking, fax, copier, & private phones, carriage rides can be arranged
RESTRICTIONS	No smoking. No pets. Children under 15 discouraged
AWARDS	17 awards for excellence, including: 50 Best Inns of the Year, *Inn Times*, 1991 12 Best B&B's, *Adventure Road*, 1991 Top 10 B&B's, *The Inndependent*, 1991
REVIEWED	*America's Wonderful Little Hotels & Inns* *B&B American Style* *The Colorado B&B Guide* *The Colorado Guide* *Frommer's Denver, Boulder, & Colorado Springs* *Inspected, Rated & Approved B&B's* *Recommended Country Inns of the Rocky Mountain Region*
RSO	B&B Rocky Mountains
MEMBER	American B&B Assn. Colorado Hotel and Motel Assn. Distinctive Inns of Colorado International Inn Society Professional Assn. of Innkeepers International
RATED	AAA 3 Diamonds Mobil 3 Stars ABBA 4 Crowns INNS 5 Globes

VICTORIA OAKS INN

1575 Race St.   Denver, CO 80206   (303) 355-1818
Clyde Stephens, Resident Owner

LOCATION	1 mi. east of downtown, in Historic Capitol Hill District, just north of Colfax
OPEN	All Year
DESCRIPTION	1897 Denver Square Eclectic furnishings
NO. OF ROOMS	1 w/private bath 8 w/shared baths
RATES	PB/$69-79 SB/$39-59 Inquire about group discounts Reservation/cancellation policy
CREDIT CARDS	American Express, Diner's Club, Discover, MasterCard, Visa
BREAKFAST	Continental plus, served in dining room Catering arrangements available
AMENITIES	TV/radio/phone in rooms, 2 rooms w/fireplaces, complimentary beverages, concierge, meeting & special occasion facilities, kitchen & laundry privileges
RESTRICTIONS	None
REVIEWED	*Colorado B&B Guide* *Colorado Guide* *Frommer's Denver, Boulder & Colorado Springs*
RATED	Mobil 2 Stars

DILLON
(SUMMIT COUNTY)

A year-round resort town on the shores of Lake Dillon and a mecca for water-sport activities. Not to be missed is the August sailing regatta. From Denver, 70 miles west on I-70 and SR 6.

ANNABELLE'S BED & BREAKFAST

Box 147D Montezuma Rt.   382 Vail Circle   Dillon, CO 80435
Ann & Tim Mealey, Resident Owners   (303) 468-8667

LOCATION	In Summit Cove area, 2 mi. west of Keystone via Swan Mountain Rd. & Summit Dr.
OPEN	All Year
DESCRIPTION	1980 Mountain Home French country & eclectic furnishings
NO. OF ROOMS	2-bedroom suite w/private bath, kitchen, living room & private entrance
RATES	Summer/$50-90 Winter/$70-110 Reservation/cancellation policy
CREDIT CARDS	MasterCard, Visa
BREAKFAST	Continental plus, served in guest suite kitchen Picnic baskets available
AMENITIES	TV/radio/phone in suite, daily maid service, laundry facilities, ski storage, babysitting & crib, free swimming, Jacuzzi & sauna facilities available close by
RESTRICTIONS	No smoking. Small pets OK (resident cats)
RSO	B&B Rocky Mountains B&B Vail Valley
MEMBER	Summit County B&B Assn.

DAVE'S BED & BREAKFAST

PO Box 621   0698 Vail Circle   Dillon, CO 80435   (303) 468-2968
Dave Joslin, Resident Owner

LOCATION	In Summit Cove area, 2-1/2 mi. west of Keystone
OPEN	Thanksgiving-Easter
DESCRIPTION	1970 Contemporary A-frame
NO. OF ROOMS	3 w/2 shared baths
RATES	$50-65 Reservation/cancellation policy
CREDIT CARDS	No
BREAKFAST	Full, served in dining room Special Thanksgiving & Christmas dinners
AMENITIES	Stone fireplace, kitchen facilities available in evening, complimentary wine & cheese
RESTRICTIONS	No smoking. No pets
MEMBER	Summit County B&B Assn.

HOME & HEARTH

PO Box 891   Dillon, CO 80435   (303) 468-5541
Trudy & Bruce Robinson, Resident Owners

LOCATION	Rural neighborhood
OPEN	All Year
DESCRIPTION	1973 Traditional Antique & rustic furnishings
NO. OF ROOMS	5 w/3 shared baths
RATES	Summer/$20-35 Winter/$30-50
CREDIT CARDS	No
BREAKFAST	Full, served in dining room
AMENITIES	Hot tub, complimentary refreshments, private fishing, studio available for meetings
RESTRICTIONS	Smoking limited. Resident dogs
RSO	Summit Central Reservations
MEMBER	Summit County B&B Assn.

PARADOX LODGE

5040 Montezuma Rd.   Dillon, CO 80435   (303) 468-9445
Mailing address: #35 Montezuma Rd.   Dillon, CO 80435
George & Connie O'Bleness, Resident Owners

LOCATION	5 mi. east of Keystone in the Snake River Valley
OPEN	All Year
DESCRIPTION	1987 Contemporary Country On 37 acres Antique & country furnishings
NO. OF ROOMS	4 w/shared baths 3 cabins w/private baths

RATES	Rooms/$50-90 Cabins/$75-120 Reservation/cancellation policy 3-night minimum stay at Christmas
CREDIT CARDS	American Express, MasterCard, Visa
BREAKFAST	Continental plus, served in dining room
AMENITIES	Wood stoves in rooms, complimentary seasonal refreshments, private fishing on Snake River
RESTRICTIONS	Smoking limited. Pets in cabins only
REVIEWED	*Colorado B&B Guide*
RSO	B&B Rocky Mountains Summit County Central Reservations

SNOWBERRYHILL BED & BREAKFAST

PO Box 2910   Dillon, CO 80435   (303) 468-8010
George & Kristi Blincoe, Resident Owners

LOCATION	Between Dillon & Keystone
OPEN	All Year
DESCRIPTION	1984 3-Story Contemporary Colonial Antique furnishings
NO. OF ROOMS	2-room suite w/private bath & kitchen
RATES	Summer/$65 Winter/$90-110 Reservation/cancellation policy
CREDIT CARDS	MasterCard, Visa
BREAKFAST	Full gourmet, served in dining room or suite Special diets accommodated with notice
AMENITIES	Private entrance, TV/VCR/phone in suite, daily maid service, full kitchen, ski locker, laundry facilities, crib/baby equipment available
RESTRICTIONS	No smoking. No pets
RSO	B&B Rocky Mountains
MEMBER	Summit County B&B Assn.

SWAN MOUNTAIN INN

Through Reservation Service Only:
PO Box 491   Vail, CO 81658   (303) 949-1212   (800) 748-2666

LOCATION	7 mi. northwest of Breckenridge
OPEN	All Year
DESCRIPTION	Log Home Rustic furnishings
NO. OF ROOMS	2 w/private baths 2 w/shared bath
RATES	$40-120 Reservation/cancellation policy 2-night minimum in winter
CREDIT CARDS	American Express, MasterCard, Visa
BREAKFAST	Full or continental, served in dining room or guestrooms Dinner & lunch available
AMENITIES	Hot tub/sauna, TV/radio/phone in rooms, complimentary refreshments, meeting facilities, handicapped access
RESTRICTIONS	No smoking. No pets. Children over 10
RSO	B&B Assn. of Vail/Ski Areas

DIVIDE

A small mountain community in the Ute Pass area, 7 miles west of Woodland Park, and 30 miles west of Colorado Springs via Hwy. 24. This is the main access route to Cripple Creek. Handy to Penetente Canyon for world-class rock climbing, and 7.5 miles from Mueller State Park.

SILVERWOOD BED & BREAKFAST

463 County Rd. 512   Divide, CO 80814   (719) 687-6784
Lawrence & Bess Oliver, Resident Owners

LOCATION	4 mi. northwest of only traffic light on paved County Road
OPEN	All Year
DESCRIPTION	1991 Contemporary Southwestern furnishings
NO. OF ROOMS	2 w/private baths
RATES	$65-75 Reservation/cancellation policy
CREDIT CARDS	No
BREAKFAST	Full, served in dining room Special meals also available
AMENITIES	TV/radio in rooms, private decks, complimentary refreshments
RESTRICTIONS	No smoking. No pets (resident cats). No children
MEMBER	B&B Innkeepers of Colorado

DOLORES

In the southwest Four Corners area, 11 miles northeast of Cortez via Hwys. 145 &
160, on the Dolores River. Site of McPhee Reservoir, and gateway to the San Juan
Skyway Scenic Loop.

MOUNTAIN VIEW BED & BREAKFAST

28050 County Rd. P   Dolores, CO 81323   *(303) 882-7861*
Cecil & Brenda Dunn, Resident Owners   *(800) 228-4592*

LOCATION	1 mi. east of Hwy. 145, 1/2 way between Cortez & Dolores, in Old Stoner Ski Area
OPEN	All Year
DESCRIPTION	1984 Country On 22 acres Country furnishings
NO. OF ROOMS	3 w/private baths 3 family suites w/private baths 2-bedroom cottage w/private bath
RATES	Rooms/$35-45 Suites/$55 Cottage/$75 Reservation/cancellation policy
CREDIT CARDS	Discover, MasterCard, Visa
BREAKFAST	Full, served in dining room, on porch or deck Lunch & dinner available by reservation
AMENITIES	TV/radio in game room, complimentary refreshments, guest laundry, facilities for meetings, workshops, retreats & reunions, handicapped access
RESTRICTIONS	No smoking. No pets (resident horses). No alcoholic beverages
RSO	B&B Rocky Mountains

Rio Grande Southern Hotel

PO Box 516   101 S. 5th   Dolores, CO 81323   (303) 882-7527
Beverly & Tom Clark, Resident Owners

LOCATION	On Town Square
OPEN	All Year
DESCRIPTION	Historic 1893 Railroad Hotel Victorian furnishings National Historic Register
NO. OF ROOMS	2 w/private baths 11 w/shared baths
RATES	PB/$36-42 SB/$32-39 Reservation/cancellation policy
CREDIT CARDS	American Express, Diner's Club, Discover, MasterCard, Visa
BREAKFAST	Full, served in dining room Lunch & dinner available in restaurant
AMENITIES	Pre-breakfast coffee & pastry brought to rooms
RESTRICTIONS	No pets
LISTED	*A Treasury of Bed & Breakfast*
MEMBER	American B&B Assn.

Stoner Lodge

25134 Hwy. 145   Dolores, CO 81323   (303) 882-7825
Kevin & Tammy Wright, Resident Managers

LOCATION	14 mi. northeast of Dolores on Hwy. 145, 1/4 mi. from Dolores River
OPEN	May 1-Jan. 1
DESCRIPTION	1954 Log Lodge w/Restaurant Rustic furnishings
NO. OF ROOMS	3 w/private baths 7 w/shared baths
RATES	PB/$35-45 SB/$30-40 Reservation/cancellation policy
CREDIT CARDS	MasterCard, Visa
BREAKFAST	Full, served in dining room Dinner available in restaurant
AMENITIES	Common room with pool table
RESTRICTIONS	None. Resident cat & dog
REVIEWED	*The Colorado Guide*

DURANGO

A natural southwest gateway to one of the most scenic areas of the state, surrounded by the awesome, jagged San Juan Mountains. In summer, it is connected to Silverton by the Durango & Silverton Narrow Gauge Railroad over 45 miles of spectacular scenery. Most direct route from Denver is via I-25 and Hwy. 160.

BLUE LAKE RANCH

16919 Hwy. 140   Hesperus, CO 81326   (303) 385-4537
David & Shirley Alford, Resident Owner

LOCATION	16 mi. west of Durango via Hwy. 160 & 140, near La Plata Mountains & River
OPEN	All Year
DESCRIPTION	1910 Homestead w/French Country addition, lakeside cabin & cottage in the woods On 100 acres French Country furnishings
NO. OF ROOMS	4 w/private baths in main Inn 3 rooms in cabin w/2 baths & fully-equipped kitchen 1 room in cottage w/private bath
RATES	Main Inn: Dbl/$85-150 Sgl/$75-125 Cabin/$195 Cottage/$150 $25 each additional person 2-night minimum Reservation/cancellation policy Map sent w/confirmation
CREDIT CARDS	No
BREAKFAST	Full European buffet, served in dining room
AMENITIES	Hot tub, robes, fireplaces in some rooms, TV/radio/phones in rooms, complimentary afternoon tea, 3-acre trout filled lake
RESTRICTIONS	No smoking. No pets (resident cat & dog)
REVIEWED	*The Colorado B&B Guide*
RSO	B&B Rocky Mountains Durango Area Chamber Resort Assn. Off the Beaten Path
MEMBER	B&B Innkeepers of Colorado Colorado Hotel and Motel Assn.

BLUE SPRUCE TRADING POST

13544 County Rd. 240   Durango, CO 81301   (303) 259-5657
Roy & Hennie Bell, Resident Owners

LOCATION	13 mi. northeast of Durango
OPEN	May-Nov.
DESCRIPTION	1975 Log Lodge w/Restaurant Contemporary furnishings
NO. OF ROOMS	5 w/private baths
RATES	$30-40 Reservation/cancellation policy
CREDIT CARDS	American Express, MasterCard, Visa
BREAKFAST	Full, served in dining room Lunch & dinner available in restaurant
AMENITIES	Restaurant/tavern, laundry facilities
RESTRICTIONS	No smoking. No pets
RSO	B&B Rocky Mountains

COUNTRY SUNSHINE
BED & BREAKFAST

35130 Hwy. 550 North   Durango, CO 81301   *(303) 247-2853*
Jim & Jill Anderson, Resident Owners   *(800) 383-2853*

LOCATION	12 mi. north of Durango, .7 mi. north of Durango Realty Office, right turn
OPEN	May 1-October 31
DESCRIPTION	1979 Ranch Rustic furnishings
NO. OF ROOMS	4 w/private baths 3 w/shared baths

RATES	PB/$65-70 SB/$50-55
	Reservation/cancellation policy
CREDIT CARDS	MasterCard, Visa
BREAKFAST	Full, served in dining room
AMENITIES	Common room w/pool table, TV/VCR, fireplaces in some rooms, complimentary refreshments, kitchen/laundry facilities
RESTRICTIONS	No smoking. No pets. Children 5 & older
REVIEWED	*B&B U.S.A.*
	Colorado B&B Guide
MEMBER	B&B Innkeepers of Colorado
RATED	Mobil 2 Stars

GABLE HOUSE

805 E. 5th Ave.   Durango, CO 81301   (303) 247-4982
Heather & Jeffrey Bryson, Resident Owners   FAX: (303) 259-1823

LOCATION	5 blocks east of downtown & Narrow Gauge Railroad Station
OPEN	June-Aug.
DESCRIPTION	1882 Queen Anne
	Antique furnishings
NO. OF ROOMS	2 w/shared bath
RATES	$45-55
	Reservation/cancellation policy
CREDIT CARDS	No
BREAKFAST	Full, served in dining room
AMENITIES	TV/radio in rooms, complimentary refreshments
RESTRICTIONS	No smoking. No pets. Children over 12
RSO	B&B Rocky Mountains

LOGWOOD/THE VERHEYDEN INN

35060 Hwy. 550 N. Durango, CO 81301 (303) 259-4396
Greg & Debby Verheyden, Resident Owners

LOCATION	13 mi. north of Durango & 13 mi. south of Purgatory Ski Area
OPEN	All Year
DESCRIPTION	1988 Western Red Cedar Log House On the Animas River Country furnishings
NO. OF ROOMS	5 w/private baths
RATES	$55-75
CREDIT CARDS	MasterCard, Visa
BREAKFAST	Full, served in dining room Christmas & New Year's dinners available
AMENITIES	Deck, complimentary afternoon & evening refreshments
RESTRICTIONS	No smoking. No pets. Children over 7
REVIEWED	*Colorado B&B Guide*
MEMBER	B&B Innkeepers of Colorado Colorado Hotel and Motel Assn.
RATED	AAA 4 Diamonds

PENNY'S PLACE

1041 County Rd. 307   Durango, CO 81301   (303) 247-8928
Penny O'Keefe, Resident Owner

LOCATION	11 mi. southeast of Durango, 1 mi. south of Hwy. 172
OPEN	All Year
DESCRIPTION	1972 Cape Cod On 27 acres Country & some antique furnishings
NO. OF ROOMS	1 w/private bath 2 w/shared bath
RATES	PB/$60-75 SB/$40-55 Reservation/cancellation policy
CREDIT CARDS	MasterCard, Visa
BREAKFAST	Full, served in dining room
AMENITIES	Solarium w/hot tub, private deck, satellite TV & fireplace in common room, radio in rooms, laundry/kitchen facilities
RESTRICTIONS	No smoking. No pets (Resident dog). Inquire about children
RSO	B&B Rocky Mountains
MEMBER	B&B Innkeepers of Colorado Colorado Hotel and Motel Assn.

RIVER HOUSE BED & BREAKFAST

495 Animas View Dr.   Durango, CO 81301   (303) 247-4775
Crystal Carroll, Resident Owner

LOCATION	1/4 mi. east of Hwy. 550. 1 mi. off County Rd. 203
OPEN	All Year
DESCRIPTION	1960 Ranch Eclectic furnishings
NO. OF ROOMS	6 w/private baths
RATES	$40-65 Reservation/cancellation policy
CREDIT CARDS	MasterCard, Visa
BREAKFAST	Full, served in Atrium, dining room or guestrooms Other meals by arrangement Special diets accommodated
AMENITIES	Living area w/wet bar, fireplace, game room, snooker table, large screen TV/VCR, exercise room, complimentary afternoon refreshments, massage therapy & hypnotherapy available, facilities for weddings, classes, retreats, reunions & private parties
RESTRICTIONS	No smoking. No pets
REVIEWED	*A Journey to the High Southwest* *A Treasury of Bed & Breakfast*
RSO	B&B Rocky Mountains
MEMBER	American B&B Assn.
RATED	ABBA 3 Crowns

Blue Sign . 1 ½ to left . Look for Iron Horse Inn
Animas

 # 6.
 # 55

SCRUBBY OAKS BED & BREAKFAST

1901 Florida Rd.   PO Box 1047   Durango, CO 81302
Mary Ann Craig, Resident Owner   (303) 247-2176

LOCATION	2.9 mi. east of 15th & Main
OPEN	10 months/year, closed November & April
DESCRIPTION	1970 Ranch House On 10 acres in the Animas Valley Antique furnishings & art work
NO. OF ROOMS	3 w/private baths 4 w/shared baths
RATES	PB/$50-65 SB/$40-55 Reservation/cancellation policy
CREDIT CARDS	No
BREAKFAST	Full gourmet, served in dining room Sack lunches available w/advance notice
AMENITIES	Cable TV/VCR, pool table & fireplace in common room, sauna, complimentary afternoon refreshments, patios, gardens, small meeting facilities, gift shop
RESTRICTIONS	No smoking. No pets (resident dog).
REVIEWED	*B&B U.S.A.* *Colorado B&B Guide* *A Treasury of B&B*
RSO	B&B Colorado
MEMBER	American B&B Assn. B&B Innkeepers of Colorado Colorado Hotel and Motel Assn.

VAGABOND INN BED & BREAKFAST

2180 Main Ave.   Durango, CO 81301   (303) 259-5901
Ace & Mary Lou Hall, Resident Owners

LOCATION	Center of town
OPEN	All Year
DESCRIPTION	1982 New England Roadhouse Provincial furnishings
NO. OF ROOMS	8 w/private baths
RATES	$43-130 Reservation/cancellation policy
CREDIT CARDS	American Express, Carte Blanche, Diner's Club, Discover, MasterCard, Visa
BREAKFAST	Continental, served in dining room
AMENITIES	Outdoor jacuzzi, 1 room w/fireplace, bridal suite w/heart-shaped hot tub, 2 rooms w/waterbeds, TV in rooms, phone available, fireplace in common area, complimentary refreshments during holidays, small meeting/reception facilities, handicapped access
RESTRICTIONS	No pets
MEMBER	B&B Guest Houses & Inns of Americas Colorado Hotel and Motel Assn.

EATON

A suburb of Greeley, 8 miles north on Hwy. 85, and handy to the Pawnee National Grasslands.

THE VICTORIAN VERANDA

515 Cheyenne Ave.   PO Box 361   Eaton, CO 80615   (303) 454-3890
Dick & Nadine White, Resident Owners

LOCATION	From stop light, west 3 blocks, then north 5-1/2 blocks, on right side
OPEN	All Year
DESCRIPTION	1894 2-Story Queen Anne Victorian with wraparound porch Antique furnishings
NO. OF ROOMS	1 w/private bath 2 w/shared bath
RATES	PB/$45-55 SB/$35-40 Reservation/cancellation policy
CREDIT CARDS	No
BREAKFAST	Full, served in dining room, guestrooms, or on veranda
AMENITIES	Jaccuzi tub in 1 room, black marble fireplace in 1 room, TV/ radio in rooms on request, outdoor fireplace/grill, complimentary refreshments, small meeting facilities, bicycles built for 2
RESTRICTIONS	No smoking. No pets. No single couples please
REVIEWED	*B&B USA* *B&B of North America* *Feather Beds & Flapjacks*
RSO	Small Luxury Hotels

EDWARDS
(VAIL/BEAVER CREEK)

Another nice alternative to spendy resorts. About 15 miles west of Vail via I-70 & Hwy. 6, and just down the road from Beaver Creek.

AUNT EM'S B&B

Through Reservation Service Only:
PO Box 491   Vail, CO 81658   (303) 949-1212   (800) 748-2666

LOCATION	3 mi. west of Beaver Creek
OPEN	All Year
DESCRIPTION	1986 Contemporary Antique furnishings
NO. OF ROOMS	1 w/private bath
RATES	Summer/$35-45 Winter/$55-65 Reservation/cancellation policy 2-night minimum in winter
CREDIT CARDS	MasterCard, Visa
BREAKFAST	Full, served in guestroom Lunch available on request
AMENITIES	Swimming pool, hot tub/sauna, TV/radio/phone in rooms
RESTRICTIONS	No smoking. No pets (resident cat). Inquire about children
RSO	B&B Assn. of Vail/Ski Areas

THE LODGE AT CORDILLERA

PO Box 1110   2205 Cordillera Way   Edwards, CO 81632
(303) 926-2200   (800) 877-3529   FAX: (303) 926-2486
Bill Clinkenbeard, Managing Partner

LOCATION	From Hwy. 6, take Squaw Creek Rd. to Cordellera Way
OPEN	All Year
DESCRIPTION	1989 European Lodge
NO. OF ROOMS	28 w/private baths
RATES	$150-400 Reservation/cancellation policy 2-night minimum on weekends and holidays
CREDIT CARDS	American Express, Diner's Club, MasterCard, Visa
BREAKFAST	Continental, served in dining room or guestrooms Lunch & dinner available
AMENITIES	Swimming pool, hot tub/sauna, robes, TV/radio/phone in rooms, fireplace in most rooms, meeting facilities, handicapped access
RESTRICTIONS	No pets. No smoking
RSO	Small Luxury Hotels
RATED	AAA 4 Diamonds

123

Eldora

A National Historic District and ski area, 21 miles west of Boulder via Hwy. 119 (Canyon Blvd.). Popular for its night skiing.

Goldminer Hotel

601 Klondyke Ave. Eldora, CO 80466   *(800) 422-4629*
Scott Bruntjen, Resident Owner   *FAX: (303) 258-7017*

LOCATION	3 mi. west of Hwy. 119, in National Historic District
OPEN	All Year
DESCRIPTION	1897 Log Miners Hotel Goldrush Period furnishings National Historic Register
NO. OF ROOMS	3 w/private baths 6 w/shared baths
RATES	PB/$55-90 SB/$43-55 Reservation/cancellation policy
CREDIT CARDS	MasterCard, Visa
BREAKFAST	Full, served in dining area
AMENITIES	Hot tub, radios in rooms, phone in some rooms, complimentary use of X-country skis, back country tours, meeting facilities, handicapped access
RESTRICTIONS	Inquire about smoking, children & pets (resident dog)

EMPIRE

Small community near Georgetown, at the foot of Berthoud Pass, 43 miles west of Denver via I-70 exit 232.

MAD CREEK BED & BREAKFAST

PO Box 404   167 Park Ave.   Empire, CO 80438   (303) 569-2003
Mike & Heather Lopez, Resident Owner

LOCATION	On main street of town, 2 mi. off I-70, Exit 232, at base of Berthod Pass
OPEN	All Year
DESCRIPTION	1881 2-Story Gothic Victorian & country/rustic furnishings
NO. OF ROOMS	2 w/shared bath
RATES	$35-45 Reservation/cancellation policy
CREDIT CARDS	No
BREAKFAST	Continental plus, served in dining room
AMENITIES	Robes, ceiling fans, rock fireplace, cable TV/VCR, books in common area, complimentary refreshments
RESTRICTIONS	Pets w/prior approval (resident dog)
RSO	B&B Rocky Mountains

THE PECK HOUSE

PO Box 428   83 Sunny Ave.   Empire, CO 80438   (303) 569-9870
Gary & Sally St. Clair, Resident Owners

LOCATION	Center of town, I-70 Exit 232
OPEN	All Year
DESCRIPTION	1860-62 Victorian Stage Coach House w/restaurant Victorian furnishings
NO. OF ROOMS	9 w/private baths 2 w/shared bath
RATES	PB/$60-80 SB/$45 Reservation/cancellation policy Inquire about minimum stay during holidays
CREDIT CARDS	American Express, Carte Blanche, Diner's Club, JCB, MasterCard, Visa
BREAKFAST	Continental, served in dining room Brunch available on Sunday
AMENITIES	Hot tub/spa, lounge, full-service restaurant, small meeting facilities
RESTRICTIONS	No pets (resident critters: dog, cat, horses, goats, donkeys)
REVIEWED	*The Best Bed & Breakfasts and Country Inns West* *The Colorado Guide* *Country Inns: Midwest & Rocky Mountain States* *The Official Guide to American Historic Inns* *Recommended Country Inns of the Rocky Mountain Region*
RSO	Treadway Reservations Service
AWARDS	Finalist, Uncle Ben's Best of Country Inns, 1991
MEMBER	Historic Hotel Assn. of the Rocky Mountain West
RATED	AAA 2 Diamonds

Estes Park

The eastern entrance to Rocky Mountain National Park, 65 miles northwest of Denver via I-25 and Hwy. 36 (Boulder Turnpike), and 40 miles north of Boulder. One of the most popular year-round visitor areas in the nation. Check out the Scottish Highland Festival in September, and listen to the routing and bugling of Elk in the fall.

The Anniversary Inn

1060 Mary's Lake Rd., Moraine Rt.   Estes Park, CO 80517
Don & Susan Landwer, Resident Owners   (303) 586-6200

LOCATION	1.5 mi. south of Hwy. 36, west side of Estes Park
OPEN	All Year
DESCRIPTION	1890 Log Home Antique & country furnishings
NO. OF ROOMS	1 w/private bath 3 w/shared baths 1 cottage w/private bath, fireplace, double whirlpool tub
RATES	PB/$76.50-110 SB/$63-75 Reservation/cancellation policy 2-night minimum for private baths
CREDIT CARDS	MasterCard, Visa
BREAKFAST	Full, served in glassed in porch
AMENITIES	Robes, TV/radio, library, games & puzzles, fireplace in living room, complimentary refreshments, wedding, reception & small meeting facilities, limited handicapped access
RESTRICTIONS	No smoking. No pets (resident dog). No children
REVIEWED	*Best Bed & Breakfasts & Country Inns: West* *Recommended Country Inns of the Rocky Mountain Region*
RSO	B&B Rocky Mountains
MEMBER	B&B Innkeepers of Colorado B&B Inns of Estes Park Professional Assn. of Innkeepers International

THE BALDPATE INN

4900 S. Highway 7   Estes Park, CO 80517   (303) 586-6151
Mike & Lois Smith, Resident Owners

LOCATION	7 mi. south of Estes Park on Hwy. 7, adjacent to Lily Lake Visitor Center, Rocky Mountain National Park
OPEN	Late May-October 1st
DESCRIPTION	1917 "Stick Style" Mountain Lodge w/restaurant Antique & log/stick furnishings
NO. OF ROOMS	2 w/private baths 10 share 5 baths 1 2-bedroom cabin w/private bath 1 3-bedroom cabin w/private bath & fireplace
RATES	PB/$65-75 SB/$50-60 Cabins/$100-125
CREDIT CARDS	MasterCard, Visa
BREAKFAST	Full, served in dining area Other meals available in restaurant
AMENITIES	TV & games in library, fireplaces in dining room, living room & library, meeting facilities, limited handicapped access, complimentary evening refreshments, famous key collection
RESTRICTIONS	No smoking. No pets (resident dog)
MEMBER	B&B Inns of Estes Park Estes Park Accommodations Assn.

BLACK DOG INN

PO Box 4659   650 S. St. Vrain Ave.   Estes Park, CO 80517
Jane & Pete Princehorn, Resident Owners   (303) 586-0374

LOCATION	1/2 mi. south of Holiday Inn on Hwy. 7, on left, 1st driveway south of Graves Ave.
OPEN	All Year
DESCRIPTION	1910 Rambling Mountain Home Antique & Native American furnishings

NO. OF ROOMS	2 w/private baths 2 w/shared bath
RATES	PB/$65-70 SB/$45-60 Reservation/cancellation policy
CREDIT CARDS	MasterCard, Visa
BREAKFAST	Full, served in dining room
AMENITIES	1 room w/TV/radio/phone & fireplace, fireplace in living room, bicycles, complimentary refreshments
RESTRICTIONS	No smoking. No pets. Children over 15. No cooking
RSO	B&B Rocky Mountains
MEMBER	B&B Innkeepers of Colorado

EAGLE CLIFF HOUSE, A BED & BREAKFAST

PO Box 4312   2383 Hwy. 66   Estes Park, CO 80517   (303) 586-5425
Nancy & Mike Conrin, Resident Owners

LOCATION	West side of Estes Park, 3/4 mi. east of YMCA of the Rockies, walking distance from Rocky Mountain National Park
OPEN	April 15-Jan. 15
DESCRIPTION	1949 Cabin Antique furnishings
NO. OF ROOMS	2 w/shared bath 1 cabin w/kitchen
RATES	Room/$45 Cabin/$75 Reservation/cancellation policy
CREDIT CARDS	No
BREAKFAST	Full, served in dining room
AMENITIES	TV/radio in rooms, complimentary bedtime snacks, wine & cheese on Sat. evenings
RESTRICTIONS	No smoking. No pets (resident dog)

HEARTHSIDE INN BED & BREAKFAST

PO Box 442   Estes Park, CO 80517-0442   (303) 586-3100
Henri & Jeanne LaVigne, Resident Owners

LOCATION	Center of town, north of Hwy. 34 on Big Horn Dr.
OPEN	All Year
DESCRIPTION	1928 European Alpine Chalet French Country furnishings
NO. OF ROOMS	3 w/private baths
RATES	$90-110 Reservation/cancellation policy 2-night minimum 3-night minimum on holidays
CREDIT CARDS	Not preferred
BREAKFAST	Full, served in dining room
AMENITIES	Fireplaces & whirlpools in rooms, robes, turn down & chambermaid service, club room w/TV, phone, wood-burning stove, books & games, complimentary refreshments, small meeting facilities
RESTRICTIONS	No smoking. No pets. Children over 15
MEMBER	B&B Inns of Estes Park

HENDERSON HOUSE

PO Box 3134   5455 Hwy. 36   Estes Park, CO 80517   (303) 586-4639
Vicki Henderson, Resident Owner

LOCATION	5 mi. southeast of Estes Park & Rocky Mountain National Park
OPEN	All Year
DESCRIPTION	1989 Victorian Victorian furnishings
NO. OF ROOMS	3 w/private bath
RATES	$105-125 Reservation/cancellation policy
CREDIT CARDS	MasterCard, Visa
BREAKFAST	Full, served in dining room
AMENITIES	Robes, complimentary refreshments, meeting facilities
RESTRICTIONS	No smoking. No pets (resident dogs & cats). No children. No single couples

RiverSong Bed & Breakfast Inn

PO Box 1910   Estes Park, CO 80517   (303) 586-4666
Gary & Sue Mansfield, Resident Owners

LOCATION	Near south entrance to Rocky Mountain National Park. From Hwy. 36, south on Mary's Lake Rd., then 1st right after crossing Big Thompson River, to end of road
OPEN	All Year
DESCRIPTION	1920's Craftsman (4 bldgs.) 30 acres on Big Thompson River
NO. OF ROOMS	9 w/private baths
RATES	$75-150 Reservation/cancellation policy 2-night minimum 3-night minimum on holidays
CREDIT CARDS	MasterCard, Visa
BREAKFAST	Full, served in dining room Dinner available by reservation
AMENITIES	4 rooms w/whirlpool baths, 8 rooms w/fireplaces, robes, complimentary refreshments, small meeting facilities, limited handicapped access
RESTRICTIONS	No smoking. No pets. Children 12 & over
REVIEWED	*The Colorado Guide* *Country Inns & Back Roads* *Recommended Country Inns of the Rocky Mountain Region*
RSO	B&B Rocky Mountains
MEMBER	Distinctive Inns of Colorado Independent Innkeepers Assn. Professional Assn. of Innkeepers International
RATED	AAA 4 Diamonds

Sapphire Rose Inn

PO Box 3663   215 Virginia Dr.   Estes Park, CO 80517   (303) 586-6607
Harry & Nancy Marsden, Resident Owners

LOCATION	Center of town, 1 block north of Hwy. 36, right turn at 2nd stoplight
OPEN	All Year
DESCRIPTION	1909 Victorian Victorian furnishings
NO. OF ROOMS	5 w/private baths 4 w/shared baths
RATES	PB/$85-120 SB/$60 Reservation/cancellation policy
CREDIT CARDS	No
BREAKFAST	Full gourmet, served in dining room Dinner available at extra charge
AMENITIES	1 room w/hot tub/sauna, robes, TV/radio & fireplaces in rooms
RESTRICTIONS	No smoking. No pets (resident dogs)

Shining Mountains Inn

PO Box 3100   775 W. Wonderview Ave.   Estes Park, CO 80517
(303) 586-5886   FAX: (303) 586-0527
Dean Wariner & Tad Bartimus, Resident Owners

LOCATION	1 mi. west of the intersection of Hwys. 34 & 36, on Hwy. 34 bypass
OPEN	All Year
DESCRIPTION	1899 Ranch On 5 acres Antique furnishings
NO. OF ROOMS	2 w/private baths 1 w/shared bath
RATES	PB/$75-85 SB/$55 Reservation/cancellation policy 2-night minimum stay
CREDIT CARDS	MasterCard, Visa
BREAKFAST	Full, served in sunroom
AMENITIES	Fireplace, TV/VCR & library in common area, robes and slippers, 1 room w/private entrance, complimentary proper English afternoon Tea, bedtime truffles, some recreational equipment, small meeting/wedding facilities, handicapped access
RESTRICTIONS	No smoking. No pets (resident dog & cats). No children
RSO	B&B Rocky Mountains
MEMBER	B&B Inns of Estes Park

FORT COLLINS

An agricultural, industrial, and educational center, 60 miles north of Denver via I-25. Home of Colorado State University and gateway to Roosevelt National Forest and Cache la Poudre River. Check out the Anheuser-Busch Clydesdales & Visitor Center, Horsetooth Reservoir & Lory State Park.

ELIZABETH STREET GUEST HOUSE

202 E. Elizabeth   Ft. Collins, CO 80524   (303) 493-2337
John and Sheryl Clark, Resident Owners

LOCATION	In Historic District, 1 block east of Colorado State Univ., corner of Elizabeth and Remington, I-25 to Rt. 14 exit
OPEN	All Year
DESCRIPTION	1905 2-Story American Foursquare Brick Antique furnishings
NO. OF ROOMS	1 w/private bath 2 w/shared bath
RATES	PB/$48-59 SB/$37-44 Whole house/$160 Reservation/cancellation policy
CREDIT CARDS	American Express, MasterCard, Visa
BREAKFAST	Full, served in dining room Special diets accommodated w/advance notice
AMENITIES	Desk/telephone in sitting room, TV in parlor, games/books available, guest refrigerator, airport shuttle service, complimentary refreshments
RESTRICTIONS	No smoking. No pets. Children over 10
REVIEWED	*America's Wonderful Little Hotels & Inns* *The Colorado Guide* *The Old-House Lover's Guide to Inns and Bed & Breakfast Guest Houses* *Recommended Country Inns of the Rocky Mountain Region*
RSO	B&B Rocky Mountains
MEMBER	B&B Innkeepers of Colorado Tourist House Assn.

FRISCO
(SUMMIT COUNTY)

70 miles west of Denver via I-70 Exit 201. This pretty town is a cross-country ski center and handy to three major ski resorts. Check out the Frisco Nordic Ski Center, and the Frisco Gold Rush, the biggest cross-country citizens race in the Rocky Mountains.

THE FINN INN

PO Box 1315   Frisco, CO 80443   (303) 668-5108
Bill & Edith Anttila, Resident Owners

LOCATION	1/2 mi. off I-70 Exit 201, 1/2 mi. north of Main St.
OPEN	All Year
DESCRIPTION	1970 Wood A-frame Country furnishings
NO. OF ROOMS	3 w/shared baths
RATES	Seasonal: $57-75
CREDIT CARDS	No
BREAKFAST	Full, served in dining room
AMENITIES	Hot tub, TV/radio in rooms, complimentary refreshments, small meeting facilities
RESTRICTIONS	None. Resident dog
REVIEWED	*Colorado B&B Guide*
RSO	B&B Rocky Mountains

FRISCO LODGE

321 Main St.   PO Box 1325   Frisco, CO 80443
(303) 668- 0195   (800) 279-6000   FAX: (303) 668-0149
Susan Wentworth & Bruce Knoepfel, Resident Owners

LOCATION	Corner of 4th & Main
OPEN	All Year
DESCRIPTION	1885 Tyrolean Rustic furnishings
NO. OF ROOMS	10 w/private baths 8 w/shared baths Reservation/cancellation policy Inquire about minimum stay
RATES	PB/$30-80 SB/$25-50
CREDIT CARDS	American Express, Discover, MasterCard, Visa
BREAKFAST	Continental, served in living room
AMENITIES	Hot tub, fireplace, TV/radio/phone in rooms, complimentary aprés ski, small meeting facilities
RESTRICTIONS	Smoking limited. No pets (resident dog). No children
MEMBER	Lake Dillon Resort Assn.

GALENA STREET MOUNTAIN INN

106 Galena St.   PO Box 417   Frisco, CO 80443   (303) 668-3224
Maxine Thomas, Manager

LOCATION	On First Ave. & Galena St., 1/2 block off Main St.
OPEN	All Year
DESCRIPTION	1991 Inn/Small Hotel Eclectic furnishings
NO. OF ROOMS	15 w/private baths
RATES	$70-105 Reservation/cancellation policy Minimum stay on holiday weekends/special events
CREDIT CARDS	American Express, MasterCard, Visa
BREAKFAST	In Season/Full Off-Season/Continental plus Served in dining room
AMENITIES	Hot tub/sauna, robes, TV/radio/phone in rooms, fireplaces in common rooms, complimentary refreshments, meeting facilities, handicapped access
RESTRICTIONS	No smoking. No pets. Inquire about children

THE LARK BED & BREAKFAST

109 Granite St. PO Box 1646 Frisco, CO 80443 (303) 668-5237
Mark & Roberta Fish, Resident Owners

LOCATION	At First & Granite, 1 block off Main St.
OPEN	All Year
DESCRIPTION	1972 2-Story Contemporary Contemporary furnishings
NO. OF ROOMS	3 w/private baths
RATES	PB/$55-90 SB/$45-75 Reservation/cancellation policy
CREDIT CARDS	American Express, MasterCard, Visa
BREAKFAST	Full, served in dining room or on sundeck Box lunch or gourmet picnic available w/advance notice
AMENITIES	Hot tub/sauna, robes, complimentary refreshments, small meeting facilities, limited handicapped access
RESTRICTIONS	No smoking. No pets (resident dog & cat). Children over 12
REVIEWED	*B&B of Colorado*
RSO	B&B of America B&B Rocky Mountains
MEMBER	B&B Innkeepers of Colorado Colorado Hotel and Motel Assn. Professional Assn. of Innkeepers International Summit County B&B Assn.

MarDei's Mountain Retreat

221 S. 4th St.   PO Box 1767   Frisco, CO 80443   (303) 668-5337
Deidre Wolach, Owner   Tammie Office, Manager   (303) 353-4865

LOCATION	Center of Frisco, 2 blocks south of Main St.
OPEN	All Year
DESCRIPTION	1930's Mountain Home American & European furnishings
NO. OF ROOMS	2 w/private baths 3 w/shared baths
RATES	PB/$50-100 SB/$15-65 Reservation/cancellation policy Inquire about whole house rates & Senior discounts 3-night minimum stay during high season
CREDIT CARDS	No
BREAKFAST	European continental, served in dining room
AMENITIES	Hot tub, 1 room w/fireplace & balcony, 1 room w/private entrance, slippers, TV/VCR, fireplace, games, books, magazines in common area, complimentary refreshments, ski lockups, limited handicapped access
RESTRICTIONS	No pets (resident dog)
REVIEWED	*B&B American Style* *The Colorado Guide* *Recommended Country Inns of the Rocky Mountain Region*
MEMBER	Summit County B&B Assn.

Naomi's Nook

PO Box 434   140 Little Chief Way   Frisco, CO 80443
(303) 668-3730/3954   FAX: (303) 668-760
Naomi Backlund, Resident Owner

LOCATION	From I-70 Exit 203, take Summit to Main, right to 4th, right to Miner's Creek Rd, right to Little Chief Way
OPEN	All Year

DESCRIPTION	1975 Contemporary 2-story, w/garden level Contemporary furnishings
NO. OF ROOMS	1 suite w/private bath
RATES	$35-40 Reservation/cancellation policy 2-night minimum stay
CREDIT CARDS	No
BREAKFAST	Full, served in dining room or suite
AMENITIES	TV/radio/phone, small refrigerator, private entrance, laundry facilities
RESTRICTIONS	None. Resident cats
MEMBER	Summit County B&B Assn.

OPEN BOX H BED & BREAKFAST

711 Belford   PO Box 1210   Frisco, CO 80443   (303) 668-0661
Chuck & Phyllis Hugins, Resident Owners

LOCATION	1/2 block west of the elementary school, between 7th & 8th Ave.
OPEN	All Year
DESCRIPTION	Contemporary Home Contemporary furnishings
NO. OF ROOMS	2 w/private baths
RATES	$36-69 Reservation/cancellation policy
CREDIT CARDS	American Express, MasterCard, Visa
BREAKFAST	Continental plus, served in dining room
AMENITIES	Hot tub, TV/radio/phone in rooms
RESTRICTIONS	No smoking. No pets
MEMBER	Summit County B&B Assn.

TWILIGHT INN

308 Main St.   PO Box 397   Frisco, CO 80443   (303) 668-5009
Jane Harrington & Rich Ahlquist, Resident Owners   FAX: (303) 668-3587

LOCATION	Center of Frisco
OPEN	All Year
DESCRIPTION	1987 Contemporary Log Antique & country furnishings
NO. OF ROOMS	8 w/private baths 4 w/shared baths
RATES	Summer/PB/$55-73 SB/$40-50 Winter/PB/$75-105 SB/$60-70 Reservation/cancellation policy 4-night minimum during winter holidays
CREDIT CARDS	American Express, Discover, MasterCard, Visa
BREAKFAST	Continental plus, served in fireside room
AMENITIES	Decks or balconies off most rooms, laundry room, TV in library, 2 living rooms w/fireplaces, hot tub & steam room, kitchen, locked storage area, cribs & high chairs, meeting facilities, handicapped access
RESTRICTIONS	Pets limited (resident dogs)
REVIEWED	*The Colorado Guide* *Recommended Country Inns of the Rocky Mountain Region*
RSO	B&B Rocky Mountains
MEMBER	Summit County B&B Assn. Professional Assn. of Innkeepers International

142

WOODS INN

205 S. 2nd St.   PO Box 1302   Frisco, CO 80443   (303) 668-3389
Murray Bain, Manager

LOCATION	In heart of Historic District, 1 block from Main St.
OPEN	All Year
DESCRIPTION	1938 Pine Log House Rustic furnishings
NO. OF ROOMS	7 w/shared baths
RATES	$30-65 Reservation/cancellation policy 2-night minimum during ski season 3-night minimum during Christmas
CREDIT CARDS	MasterCard, Visa
BREAKFAST	Winter/Full Summer/Continental plus Served in dining room or guestrooms Lunch available
AMENITIES	Hot tub, TV/radio/phone fireplace in common area, reading room, complimentary beverages, small meeting facilities, limited handicapped access
RESTRICTIONS	No smoking. No pets
MEMBER	Summit County B&B Assn.

GARDNER

In the San Isabel National Forest, 27 miles northwest of Walsenburg on Hwy. 69.

THE MALACHITE SCHOOL & SMALL FARM BED & BREAKFAST

8055 County Rd. 570 (Pass Creek Rd.)   ASR Box 21   *Gardner, CO 81040*
Alan Mace, Resident Manager   *(719) 746-2412*

LOCATION	6 mi. west of Gardner, Hwy. 69 to Redwing turnoff, then 1 mi. south on County Rd. 570
OPEN	All Year
DESCRIPTION	1880's Adobe Homestead Farmhouse w/contemporary solar wing 260 acre non-profit environmental working farm and school
NO. OF ROOMS	3 w/shared baths
RATES	SGL/$20 DBL/$40 Children under 10, 1/2 price
CREDIT CARDS	No
BREAKFAST	Full, served in dining room Lunch & dinner available
AMENITIES	Join in farm chores, organic gardening, plowing w/draft horses, hayrides, hiking, meeting facilities, handicapped access. Inquire about Farm Stay, Hostel & College programs
RESTRICTIONS	No smoking. No pets (resident cats & dog)
REVIEWED	*The Colorado Guide* (see Westcliffe)

GEORGETOWN

A remarkably restored Victorian mining town and National Historic District, 50 miles west of Denver on I-70. Close to Loveland Ski Area.

THE HARDY HOUSE BED & BREAKFAST INN

PO Box 0156   605 Brownell   Georgetown, CO 80444   (303) 569-3388
Sarah Schmidt, Resident Owner

LOCATION	Center of Georgetown
OPEN	All Year
DESCRIPTION	1880 Victorian Victorian furnishings
NO. OF ROOMS	4 w/private baths Reservation/cancellation policy
RATES	$47-72
CREDIT CARDS	MasterCard & Visa
BREAKFAST	Full, served in dining room
AMENITIES	Robes, TV in 2 rooms, fireplace in 1 room, complimentary refreshments, carriage & sleigh rides on request, mountain bike for 2
RESTRICTIONS	No smoking. No pets (resident cat). No children
REVIEWED	*America's Wonderful Little Hotels & Inns* *B&B U.S.A.* *Colorado B&B Guide* *The Colorado Guide* *The Complete Guide to B&B Inns & Guesthouses* *Recommended Country Inns of the Rocky Mountain Region*
RSO	B&B Rocky Mountains
MEMBER	B&B Innkeepers of Colorado

GLEN HAVEN

On the northeastern edge of Rocky Mountain National Park, about 7 miles north of Estes Park on Devil's Gulch Road.

INN OF GLEN HAVEN

PO Box 219   7468 County Rd. 43   Glen Haven, CO 80532
Tom & Sheila Sellers, Innkeepers   (303) 586-3897

LOCATION	Center of Glen Haven. 7-1/2 mi. north of Estes Park on Devil's Gulch Rd.
OPEN	May 1-Feb. 28, March & April for special events
DESCRIPTION	1919 Old West Victorian furnishings
NO. OF ROOMS	6 w/private baths 2 cabins w/private baths
RATES	$65-90
CREDIT CARDS	MasterCard, Visa
BREAKFAST	Continental, served in dining room Traditional English dinner available in restaurant Old English 12 Days of Christmas Feasts, Dec. 26-Jan. 5
AMENITIES	Fireplaces in cabins
RESTRICTIONS	No pets (resident dog)
RSO	B&B Rocky Mountains

GLENWOOD SPRINGS

At the western end of magnificent Glenwood Canyon, 160 miles west of Denver on I-70. Most famous for its natural hot springs pools and vapor caves, and a center for rafting on the Colorado River. Check out the Strawberry Days festival in June.

ADDUCCI'S INN BED & BREAKFAST

1023 Grand Ave. Glenwood Springs, CO 81601 (303) 945-9341
Virginia Adducci, Resident Owner

LOCATION	Center of town, 5 blocks south of I-70 Exit
OPEN	All Year
DESCRIPTION	1900 Victorian Antique furnishings
NO. OF ROOMS	1 w/private bath 4 w/shared baths
RATES	PB/$65 SB/$28-55 Inquire about group rates Reservation/cancellation policy
CREDIT CARDS	MasterCard, Visa
BREAKFAST	Full, served in dining area
AMENITIES	Hot tub during ski season, TV/radio in dining room, phone in parlor, complimentary refreshments, small meeting facilities
RESTRICTIONS	No smoking. No pets (resident dog & cats)
REVIEWED	*The Colorado Guide* *Let's Go U.S.A.*
RSO	Glenwood Central Reservations

THE KAISER HOUSE

932 Cooper Ave.   PO Box 1952   Glenwood Springs, CO 81601
(303) 945-8816   FAX: (303) 945-8816
Ingrid & Glen Eash, Resident Owners

LOCATION	Corner of 10th & Cooper Ave.
OPEN	All Year
DESCRIPTION	1902 Restored 3-Story Queen Ann Victorian Victorian furnishings
NO. OF ROOMS	7 w/private baths
RATES	$45-85 Reservation/cancellation policy 2-night minimum on summer & holiday weekends
CREDIT CARDS	MasterCard, Visa
BREAKFAST	Full gourmet, served in dining room, breakfast area or on patio
AMENITIES	Hot tub, private patio, TV/phone in room on request, complimentary afternoon refreshments, bus & train pick-up
RESTRICTIONS	No smoking. No pets (resident dogs). Children 8 & over
REVIEWED	*Colorado B&B Guide*
MEMBER	B&B Innkeepers of Colorado

SUNLIGHT INN

10252 County Rd. 117   Glenwood Springs, CO 81601   (303) 945-5225
Mary Lou Hollstein, Manager

LOCATION	12 mi. south of I-70 Glenwood Springs Exit 116, at base of Ski Sunlight
OPEN	All Year
DESCRIPTION	1946 Western Ranch Rustic/western furnishings
NO. OF ROOMS	18 w/private baths 5 w/shared baths
RATES	PB/$59 & up SB/$45
CREDIT CARDS	American Express, MasterCard, Visa
BREAKFAST	Continental, served in dining room
AMENITIES	Hot tub, fireplace in honeymoon suite, meeting facilities, handicapped access
RESTRICTIONS	No pets (resident dog)
RSO	Glenwood Springs Central Reservations

GOLDEN

Once the state's territorial capital, this historic city about 10 miles west of Denver via Hwy. 6 is home to the Colorado School of Mines, Coors Brewery, Golden Gate Canyon State Park.

DOVE INN

711 14th St.   Golden, CO 80401-1906   (303) 278-2209
Sue & Guy Beals, Resident Owners   FAX: (303) 278-4029

LOCATION	Center of Golden, 1 block south of downtown, near Coors Brewery & Colorado School of Mines
OPEN	All Year (Closed Dec. 24-25)
DESCRIPTION	1878-86 Victorian Modified Victorian furnishings
NO. OF ROOMS	5 w/private baths 2 w/shared shower & private 1/2 bath
RATES	PB/$41-64 SB/$44-49 Reservation/cancellation policy
CREDIT CARDS	American Express, Diner's Club, MasterCard, Visa
BREAKFAST	Full or continental, served in dining room Special diets accommodated w/notice
AMENITIES	TV/phone/air conditioning in rooms, complimentary beverages, baby crib available
RESTRICTIONS	No smoking. No pets. Married couples only, please
REVIEWED	*America's Wonderful Little Hotels & Inns* *B&B U.S.A.* *B&B Guest Houses & Inns of America*
RSO	B&B Rocky Mountains
MEMBER	American B&B Assn. B&B Innkeepers of Colorado
RATED	ABBA 1 Crown Mobil 2 Stars

THE JAMESON INN BED & BREAKFAST

1704 Illinois St.   Golden, CO 80401   (303) 278-0351
Peggy & Mark Shaw, Resident Owners

LOCATION	Corner of 17th & Illinois Sts., at the foot of Lookout Mt. on the Colorado School of Mines campus
OPEN	All Year
DESCRIPTION	1914 English Norman Cottage Antique & heirloom furnishings
NO. OF ROOMS	1 w/private bath 2 w/shared bath
RATES	PB/$55 SB/$45 Reservation/cancellation policy
CREDIT CARDS	MasterCard, Visa
BREAKFAST	Full gourmet, served in dining room or on sunporch
AMENITIES	Radio in rooms, cable TV/VCR in common area, library/office w/computer, sunporch, complimentary refreshments, turndown service
RESTRICTIONS	No smoking. No pets (resident cat). Children over 10
RSO	B&B Colorado B&B Rocky Mountains
MEMBER	B&B Innkeepers of Colorado

GRAND JUNCTION

Colorado's western gateway, at the southeastern edge of the Colorado National Monument, 258 miles west of Denver on I-70. Named for its location at the "grand junction" of the Colorado and Gunnison Rivers.

THE CIDER HOUSE

1126 Grand Ave.   Grand Junction, CO 81501   (303) 242-9087
Helen Mills, Resident Owner

LOCATION	I-70 to Horizon Dr. Exit, left on 2nd St. to Grand Ave., left on Grand
OPEN	All Year (Closed Dec. 20-27)
DESCRIPTION	1907 2-Story Frame Victorian furnishings
NO. OF ROOMS	1 w/private bath 3 w/shared bath
RATES	PB/$32-42 SB/$28-38 Reservation/cancellation policy
CREDIT CARDS	MasterCard, Visa
BREAKFAST	Full, served in dining room Picnic hampers & other meals available at extra charge
AMENITIES	Large front porch, complimentary evening cider & refreshments, shuttle service on request
RESTRICTIONS	No smoking. No pets
RSO	B&B Rocky Mountains

JUNCTION COUNTRY INN BED & BREAKFAST

861 Grand Ave.   Grand Junction, CO 81501   (303) 241-2817
Karl & Theresa Bloom, Resident Owners

LOCATION	Corner of 9th & Grand Ave.
OPEN	All Year
DESCRIPTION	1907 Classic Box Victorian furnishings
NO. OF ROOMS	2 w/private baths 2 w/shared bath
RATES	PB/$40-49 SB/$25-34 Reservation/cancellation policy
CREDIT CARDS	American Express, MasterCard, Visa
BREAKFAST	Full, served in dining room
AMENITIES	Radio in rooms, TV in some rooms, complimentary refreshments, 2 parlors, meeting/reception facilities
RESTRICTIONS	No smoking. No pets (resident dog)
RSO	B&B Rocky Mountains
MEMBER	B&B Innkeepers of Colorado Professional Assn. of Innkeepers International

THE VICTORIAN GARDEN

447 Santa Clara   Grand Junction, CO 81503   (303) 241-0466
Brent & Norma Miller, Resident Owners

LOCATION	1 mi. south of Main St. on Hwy. 50, next to Duck Pond Park
OPEN	All Year
DESCRIPTION	1932 Victorian Guesthouse Country French furnishings
NO. OF ROOMS	2 w/private baths
RATES	$45 Reservation/cancellation policy
CREDIT CARDS	No
BREAKFAST	Full, served in dining room
AMENITIES	TV/radio & fireplaces in rooms, complimentary refreshments, English Tea House & gift shop on property
RESTRICTIONS	No smoking. Resident dog & rabbit

GRAND LAKE

A resort community having Colorado's largest body of natural water and the nation's highest chartered yacht club. This snowmobile capital of Colorado, is at the west entrance to Rocky Mountain National Park, 100 miles northwest of Denver via I-70 and Hwys. 40 & 34.

ONAHU LODGE

PO Box 562   2096 County Rd. 491   Grand Lake, CO 80447
Donna Lyons, Resident Owner   (303) 627-8523

LOCATION	5 mi. north of Grand Lake, bordering Rocky Mountain National Park
OPEN	All Year
DESCRIPTION	1969 Hand-Peeled Log Ranch Western Rustic furnishings
NO. OF ROOMS	1 w/private bath 1 w/shared bath
RATES	PB/$60-75 SB/$50-60 Reservation/cancellation policy 2-night minimum stay
CREDIT CARDS	No
BREAKFAST	Continental plus, served in dining room
AMENITIES	Fireplace in living area, private patio, complimentary refreshments, small meeting/wedding facilities, handicapped access in summer only, horse corrals & horse trailer parking space
RESTRICTIONS	No smoking. Pets limited (resident horses). Children over 5
REVIEWED	*Colorado B&B Guide*
RSO	B&B Rocky Mountains

THE TERRACE INN

PO Box 647   813 Grand Ave.   Grand Lake, CO 80447   (303) 627-3079
Rob & Debby Tedesco, Resident Owners

LOCATION	Centrally located, next to Yamaha snowmobile dealership
OPEN	10 months (Closed April & Oct. 15-Nov. 15)
DESCRIPTION	1905 Victorian w/restaurant Eclectic furnishings
NO. OF ROOMS	4 w/private baths
RATES	$40-65 Reservation/cancellation policy
CREDIT CARDS	MasterCard, Visa
BREAKFAST	Full, served in dining room Other meals & trail lunches available
AMENITIES	TV/radio in rooms, lounge, small meeting facilities
RESTRICTIONS	No pets (resident dog & cat)

WINDING RIVER RESORT VILLAGE

PO Box 629   1447 County Rd. 491   Grand Lake, CO 80447
(303) 627-3215   FAX: (303) 623-1121
Wes & Sue House, Resident Owners

LOCATION	1-1/2 mi. north of Grand Lake on Hwy. 34, 1-1/2 mi. west on Rd. 491
OPEN	All Year
DESCRIPTION	1965 Log Lodge Eclectic furnishings
NO. OF ROOMS	3 w/private baths
RATES	$75 Reservation/cancellation policy
CREDIT CARDS	MasterCard, Visa
BREAKFAST	Full, served in dining room Special meals available
RESTRICTIONS	No smoking. No pets (resident dog & horses)
RSO	B&B Rocky Mountains Grand Lake Central Reservations

GREELEY

An agricultural community immortalized in *Centennial*, 54 miles northeast of Denver via I-25 and Hwy. 34. Home of the University of Northern Colorado, and the nation's largest rodeo, the Greeley Independence Stampede. Check out Centennial Village and scrimmages at the Denver Broncos Training Camp.

STERLING HOUSE BED & BREAKFAST INN

818 12th St. Greeley, CO 80631 (303) 351-8805
Lillian Peeples, Resident Owner

LOCATION	Downtown, between 8th & 9th Aves.
OPEN	All Year
DESCRIPTION	1886 Renovated Plains Victorian Antique furnishings
NO. OF ROOMS	1 w/private bath 1 suite w/private bath (can sleep 4)
RATES	$34-49 Reservation/cancellation policy
CREDIT CARDS	MasterCard, Visa
BREAKFAST	Full gourmet, served in dining room or guestrooms Dinner available
AMENITIES	Fresh fruit in rooms, fireplace in commons area, front porch swing, complimentary refreshments upon arrival, shuttle service from Denver/Stapleton airport, small meeting facilities
RESTRICTIONS	Smoking limited. No pets. Children over 10
REVIEWED	*The Colorado Guide*
RSO	B&B Rocky Mountains

GREEN MOUNTAIN FALLS
(COLORADO SPRINGS)

A charming mountain town 18 miles west of Colorado Springs with a waterfall, lake, and annual Yule Log Hunt.

OUTLOOK LODGE BED & BREAKFAST

6975 Howard St.   PO Box 5   Green Mountain Falls, CO 80819
Patrick & Hayley Moran, Resident Owners   (719) 684-2303

LOCATION	Center of town, next to Church of the Wildwood
OPEN	All Year
DESCRIPTION	1889 Victorian Victorian Country furnishings
NO. OF ROOMS	4 w/private baths 3 w/shared baths 2 suites w/private baths
RATES	Rooms/PB/$55 SB/$45 Suites/$68 Reservation/cancellation policy
CREDIT CARDS	Discover, MasterCard, Visa
BREAKFAST	Full, served in dining room
AMENITIES	Fireplace in lobby, complimentary refreshments, meeting facilities
RESTRICTIONS	No smoking. No pets (resident dog)
REVIEWED	*The Colorado Guide* *Recommended Country Inns of the Rocky Mountain Region*

GUNNISON

The eastern entrance to Curecanti National Recreational Area, which includes Blue Mesa Reservoir and Black Canyon of the Gunnison. From Denver, 196 miles southwest via Hwy. 285 and Hwy. 50 over Monarch Pass. Or 30 miles south of Crested Butte.

THE MARY LAWRENCE INN

601 N. Taylor   Gunnison, CO 81230   (303) 641-3343
Tom Bushman & Les Noble-Bushman, Resident Owners

LOCATION	Center of town, corner of Taylor & Ruby
OPEN	All Year
DESCRIPTION	1886 Renovated Italianate Eclectic w/antique furnishings
NO. OF ROOMS	3 w/private baths 2 w/shared bath
RATES	PB/$58-78 SB/$45-50 Reservation/cancellation policy
CREDIT CARDS	MasterCard, Visa
BREAKFAST	Full, served in dining room Self-serve continental for early risers Box lunch & dinner available
AMENITIES	Robes, coffee station & refrigerator, complimentary refreshments, piano, tandem bicycle, crib, sun room , deck & veranda, ski packages, special event weekends, off-street parking
RESTRICTIONS	No smoking. No pets (resident rabbit)
AWARDS	1991 Excellence in Preservation, Colorado Preservation, Inc. 1991 Top 50 Inns, *Inn Times*
REVIEWED	*America's Wonderful Little Hotels & Inns* *Colorado B&B Guide* *The Colorado Guide*
MEMBER	B&B Innkeepers of Colorado Professional Assn. of Innkeepers International

160

HOT SULPHUR SPRINGS

Known for its hot mineral pools, 94 miles northwest of Denver via I-70 and Hwy. 40.

RIVERSIDE HOTEL

509 Grand Ave.   PO Box 22   Hot Sulphur Springs, CO 80451
Abraham Renta, Resident Owner   (303) 725-3589

LOCATION	1 block north of Hwy. 40, by the Colorado River
OPEN	All Year
DESCRIPTION	1903 Western Victorian
NO. OF ROOMS	1 w/private bath 20 w/shared baths
RATES	$26-34 Reservation/cancellation policy
CREDIT CARDS	No
BREAKFAST	Continental, served in dining area Dinner & summer lunches available
AMENITIES	Handicapped access, meeting facilities
RESTRICTIONS	No pets
REVIEWED	*The Colorado Guide* *Country Inns, Lodges & Historic Hotels*

HOTCHKISS

In Gunnison country, 300 miles southwest of Denver via I-70, Hwy. 50 & 92.

YE OLE OASIS BED & BREAKFAST

3142 J Road   Hotchkiss, CO 81419   (303) 872-3794
Dwight & Rose Marie Ward, Resident Owners

LOCATION	17 mi. east of Delta on Hwy. 92, 1-1/2 mi. southeast of the Jagear turnoff, on Rogers Mesa
OPEN	April-Oct.
DESCRIPTION	1906 2-story Victorian Farmhouse Antique furnishings & family heirlooms
NO. OF ROOMS	3 w/shared baths
RATES	Sgl/$25-30 Dbl/$40-45 Reservation/cancellation policy Senior discount
CREDIT CARDS	MasterCard, Visa
BREAKFAST	Full, served in dining room or kitchen Picnic lunches available at extra charge
AMENITIES	TV/radio, complimentary refreshments
RESTRICTIONS	No smoking. No pets (resident dogs, cat & horses). Inquire about children
REVIEWED	*B&B U.S.A.* *The Colorado Guide*
RSO	B&B Rocky Mountains
MEMBER	B&B Innkeepers of Colorado

IDAHO SPRINGS

Has one of the few working underground gold mines in the state. Also more hot mineral springs, Bridal Veil Falls, and gateway to the nation's highest paved auto road to the top of Mt. Evans. From Denver, 32 miles west on I-70.

ST. MARY'S GLACIER BED & BREAKFAST

336 Crest Dr. Idaho Springs, CO 80452   (303) 567-4084
Steve & Jackie Jacquin, Resident Owners

LOCATION	10 mi. north of I-70 Exit 238, Fall River Rd.
OPEN	All Year (Full time in summer, weekends only during school year)
DESCRIPTION	Mountain Cabin
NO. OF ROOMS	1 w/private bath
RATES	$65
CREDIT CARDS	No
BREAKFAST	Full, served in dining area
AMENITIES	Private hot tub, deck, wood burning stove in living room, complimentary sherry
RESTRICTIONS	No smoking. Children over 12
RSO	B&B Rocky Mountains

KEYSTONE
(SUMMIT COUNTY)

This is a major planned, corporate-owned year-round resort area, with skiing on 3 mountains, ice skating and boating on Keystone Lake. 70 miles west of Denver on I-70.

SKI TIP LODGE

PO Box 38   0764 Montezuma Rd.   Keystone, CO 80435   (303) 468-4202
Kelly Short, Manager   (800) 222-0188

LOCATION	10 mi. east of Dillon on Hwy. 6, approx. 2 mi. on Montezuma Rd., near Keystone Resort
OPEN	All Year
DESCRIPTION	1868 & 1940's Rustic Log & Stone Lodge w/Restaurant Rustic country furnishings
NO. OF ROOMS	17 w/private baths 2 w/shared bath
RATES	Summer/$48-118 Winter/$114-228 (includes breakfast & dinner) Reservation/cancellation policy
CREDIT CARDS	American Express, Diner's Club, MasterCard, Visa
BREAKFAST	Summer/Continental plus Winter/Full breakfast & 4-course dinner Served in dining room. Winter rates include 4-course dinner Lunch available in winter
AMENITIES	Access to Keystone Resort facilities: swimming pool, whirlpool, tennis; complimentary afternoon tea in winter, small meeting facilities, limited handicapped access
RESTRICTIONS	Smoking limited. No pets
REVIEWED	*The Colorado Guide* *Recommended Country Inns of the Rocky Mountain Region*
RSO	Keystone Resort
MEMBER	Distinctive Inns of Colorado
RATED	AAA 2 Diamonds

LA VETA

At the north end of the beautiful Cuchara Valley, this quiet little town is alive with art, artists, and theatrical productions. Adjacent to the town is an 18-hole championship golf course. From Walsenburg, 14 miles west via Hwys. 160 & 12.

1899 INN BED & BREAKFAST

314 S. Main   PO Box 372   La Veta, CO 81055   (719) 742-3576
Marilyn Hall, Resident Owner

LOCATION	Center of town, next to Ft. Francisco Museum & La Veta Library
OPEN	All Year (Closed Dec. 1-25 & May)
DESCRIPTION	1909 Gabled Stone House Early American furnishings
NO. OF ROOMS	3 w/private bath 3 w/shared bath
RATES	PB/$37.50-42.50 SB/$32.50-37.50 Reservation/cancellation policy
CREDIT CARDS	No
BREAKFAST	Full, served in dining room
AMENITIES	Robes, piano, games, library, porch swing, gift shop
RESTRICTIONS	No smoking. Pets limited (resident cat)
REVIEWED	*The Colorado B&B Guide* *The Colorado Guide* *Colorado Historic Inns & Hotels* *Country Inns: Midwest/Rockies* *Inns of the Southwest* *The Official Guide to American Historic B&B Inns & Guesthouses* *The Old-House Lover's Guide to Inns and Bed & Breakfast Guest Houses* *Recommended Country Inns of the Rocky Mountain Region*
RSO	B&B Rocky Mountains
MEMBER	B&B Innkeepers of Colorado

LAKE CITY

This showplace for restored, Victorian architecture and Colorado's largest National Historic District was also the site of the infamous Alferd Packer's trial. Located at the confluence of the Lake Fork of the Gunnison River and Henson Creek, 55 miles southwest of Gunnison on Hwy. 149. Check out the Alferd Packer Jeep Tour and Barbeque in September.

THE ADOBE BED & BREAKFAST

625 Pine St.   PO Box 697   Lake City, CO 81235   (303) 944-2642
Helen & Warner Dewey, Resident Owners

LOCATION	Residential area, 4 blocks east of Hwy. 149
OPEN	June-October
DESCRIPTION	1986 Southwestern Adobe Southwestern furnishings
NO. OF ROOMS	2 share 1-1/2 baths
RATES	Sgl/$45-60 Dbl/$65-75 Reservation/cancellation policy
CREDIT CARDS	No
BREAKFAST	Full gourmet, served in dining room
AMENITIES	Hot tub, solarium, common room, robes, fireplaces in rooms, down comforters, complimentary refreshments, art gallery on premises
RESTRICTIONS	No smoking. No pets. Children over 10
RSO	B&B Rocky Mountains
MEMBER	B&B Innkeepers of Colorado

THE CINNAMON INN
BED & BREAKFAST

426 Gunnison Ave.   PO Box 533   Lake City, CO 81235
Mel & Gwen Faber, Resident Owners   (303) 944-2641

LOCATION	Center of town, corner of Hwy. 149 & 5th St.
OPEN	All Year
DESCRIPTION	1878 Victorian Colonial Country Victorian furnishings
NO. OF ROOMS	1 w/private bath 4 w/2 shared baths
RATES	PB/$85 SB/$60-70
CREDIT CARDS	MasterCard, Visa
BREAKFAST	Full gourmet, served in country kitchen or enclosed back porch Sack lunches available, dinner in winter
AMENITIES	Whirlpool, fireplaces in rooms, complimentary beverages, games/puzzles/cards/books/piano in sitting room
RESTRICTIONS	No smoking. Inquire about pets (resident cats) & children
MEMBER	B&B Innkeepers of Colorado

MONCRIEF MOUNTAIN RANCH

PO Box 593   Lake City, CO 81235   (303) 944-2796
Kristy Gunning, Manager   FAX: c/o (303) 944-2524

LOCATION	2 mi. south of town on Hwy. 149, turn right at Lake San Cristobal. At south end of lake, turn right on HC Rd. 30, 1.7 mi. to Ranch sign
OPEN	All Year (Closed June 10-July 12 for special camp)
DESCRIPTION	1981-84 Western Log w/multi-level system of decks On 320 acres Western & Victorian furnishings
NO. OF ROOMS	10 w/private baths 2 w/shared bath 2 separate dorm facilities w/4 shared baths
RATES	$55-125 Inquire about group rates Reservation/cancellation policy
CREDIT CARDS	American Express, Discover, MasterCard, Visa
BREAKFAST	Full, served in dining room, great room, guestrooms or on decks Lunch & dinner available in restaurant Barbeques & outdoor cookouts arranged Sunday Champagne Brunch
AMENITIES	Hot tub, large screen TV & ping pong table in game room, phones available, complimentary refreshments, 100 seat auditorium, decks available for activities, photo lab, handicapped access, arrangements made for group activities & excursions
RESTRICTIONS	No smoking. No pets (resident dogs, horses & pet trout)
AWARDS	1985 American Institute of Architects Honor Award, Colorado West Chapter
RSO	The Higher Elevations Co.
MEMBER	Lake City B&B Assn.

THE MOSS ROSE BED & BREAKFAST

PO Box 910   Lake City, CO 81235
Dan & Joan Moss, Resident Owners

LOCATION	In Capitol City, 9 mi. west of Lake City, on Henson Creek Rd., on the historic Lee Mansion site
OPEN	June-September
DESCRIPTION	1988 Contemporary Southwest Solar Southwestern & traditional furnishings
NO. OF ROOMS	1 w/private bath 2 w/shared bath
RATES	PB/$55 SB/$40-45
CREDIT CARDS	No
BREAKFAST	Full, served in dining room
AMENITIES	Robes, deck, complimentary refreshments, limited handicapped access
RESTRICTIONS	No smoking. No pets (resident dog). No children

OLD CARSON INN

PO Box 144   Lake City, CO 81235   (303) 944-2511
Don & Judy Berry, Resident Owners

LOCATION	11 mi. southwest of Lake City on Hinsdale County Road 30 (Alpine Loop)
OPEN	All Year
DESCRIPTION	1991 Mountain Log Home Antique furnishings
NO. OF ROOMS	5 w/private baths
RATES	$45-85 Reservation/cancellation policy
CREDIT CARDS	MasterCard, Visa
BREAKFAST	Full, served in dining room or sunroom
AMENITIES	Hot tub/sauna, satellite TV/VCR, games & books in common area, sunroom w/woodburning stove, complimentary refreshments
RESTRICTIONS	No smoking. Inquire about pets & children
MEMBER	B&B Innkeepers of Colorado

RYAN'S ROOST

9501 Hwy. 149   PO Box 218   Lake City, CO 81235   (303) 944-2339
Jim & Therese Ryan, Resident Owners

LOCATION	8 1/2 mi. north of Lake City, between mi. post 82 & 81 on Hwy. 149
OPEN	All Year
DESCRIPTION	1976 3-Level Ranch Country/heirloom furnishings
NO. OF ROOMS	3 w/private baths
RATES	$45-85 Reservation/cancellation policy
CREDIT CARDS	MasterCard, Visa
BREAKFAST	Full, served in dining room
AMENITIES	Hot tub, robes, radio in rooms, fireplace in 1 room, complimentary refreshments, limited handicapped access. Horse corrals available at additional charge
RESTRICTIONS	Smoking limited. Inquire about pets (resident cats) & children
MEMBER	B&B Innkeepers of Colorado

LEADVILLE

Once the epitome of boom-town wealth, this Historic Victorian mining town lies in the spectacular Arkansas Valley in the shadow of Colorado's two highest peaks, Mt. Elbert and Mt. Massive. Check out the fish at Turquoise Lake, Crystal Lakes, and the U.S. Fish Hatchery. From Denver 103 miles southwest on I-70 to Copper Mountain, then south 24 miles on Hwy. 91.

THE APPLE BLOSSOM INN VICTORIAN BED & BREAKFAST

120 W. 4th St.   Leadville, CO 80461   (719) 486-2141
Margaret R. Senn, Resident Owner   (800) 982-9279

LOCATION	Center of downtown, 1/2 block from Harrison Ave. (main street)
OPEN	All Year
DESCRIPTION	1879 Victorian Victorian furnishings
NO. OF ROOMS	2 w/private baths 4 w/shared baths
RATES	PB/$45-60 SB/$35-45 Reservation/cancellation policy
CREDIT CARDS	MasterCard, Visa
BREAKFAST	Full, served in dining room or guest rooms Special meals available
AMENITIES	Robes, TV/radio/phone & fireplaces in some rooms, complimentary refreshments, small meeting facilities
RESTRICTIONS	No smoking. Inquire about pets
RSO	Leadville/Twin Lakes Lodging Assn.
MEMBER	B&B Innkeepers of Colorado Professional Assn. of Innkeepers International

172

DELAWARE HOTEL

700 Harrison Ave.   Leadville, CO 80461   (719) 486-1418
Bonnie Blamey, Manager   (800) 748-2004

LOCATION	On main street, center of town
OPEN	All Year
DESCRIPTION	1886 3-Story Victorian Hotel Antique furnishings
NO. OF ROOMS	36 w/private baths
RATES	$35-50 Suites/$70-80
CREDIT CARDS	American Express, Diner's Club, Discover, MasterCard, Visa
BREAKFAST	Continental plus, served in dining room Dinner available
RESTRICTIONS	None
AMENITIES	Hot tub, TV in rooms, complimentary fruit basket
REVIEWED	*The Colorado Guide* *Recommended Country Inns of the Rocky Mountain Region*
RSO	B&B Rocky Mountains

THE LEADVILLE COUNTRY INN

127 E. 8th St.   PO Box 1989   Leadville, CO 80461   (719) 486-2354/3411
Judy & Sid Clemmer, Resident Owners   *(800) 748-2354*

LOCATION	1/2 block east of Harrison Ave., third house on right
OPEN	All Year
DESCRIPTION	1893 Queen Anne Victorian Country Victorian furnishings
NO. OF ROOMS	9 w/private baths
RATES	Sgl/$52-77 Dbl/$62-107 Reservation/cancellation policy 2-night minimum during peak season
CREDIT CARDS	American Express, Diner's Club, Discover, MasterCard, Visa
BREAKFAST	Full gourmet, served in dining area or guestrooms on request Candlelight dinner w/carriage or sleigh ride available at extra charge
AMENITIES	Jacuzzi in gazebo, robes in some rooms, TV/radio/phone in 1 room, bicycles, sleigh/carriage rides, complimentary fresh baked goods, special weekends, wedding/meeting facilities, limited handicapped access
RESTRICTIONS	No smoking. No pets. Children over 3
REVIEWED	*America's Wonderful Little Hotels & Inns* *Bed & Breakfasts & Country Inns, The Official Guide to American Historic Inns* *The Best Bed & Breakfasts & Country Inns: West* *Colorado B&B Guide* *The Colorado Guide* *Inn Places for Bed & Breakfasts*
RSO	B&B Rocky Mountains
MEMBER	B&B Innkeepers of Colorado Distinctive Inns of Colorado

MOUNTAIN MANSION

129 W. 8th St.   PO Box 1229   Leadville, CO 80461-1229   (719) 486-0655
Anna Maria & Jim Nezol, Resident Owners

LOCATION	1/2 block from Harrison St.
OPEN	All Year
DESCRIPTION	1892 3-Story Victorian Some antique furnishings
NO. OF ROOMS	2 w/private bath 2 w/shared bath
RATES	$35-55 or 4-room suite: $150 Reservation/cancellation policy
CREDIT CARDS	MasterCard, Visa
BREAKFAST	Full, Argentinian or Venezuelan, served in bed, guestrooms or dining room Other meals available
AMENITIES	Giant screen TV, 2 rooms w/fireplaces, games, books, common room w/fireplace. Inquire about Spanish language workshops
RESTRICTIONS	No smoking. Inquire about pets
REVIEWED	*B&B USA* *The Colorado Guide* *Recommended Country Inns of the Rocky Mountain Region*

PERI & ED'S MOUNTAIN HIDEAWAY

201 W. 8th St.   Leadville, CO 80461   (719) 486-0716   (800) 933-3715
Peri & Edward Solder, Resident Owners   FAX: (719) 486-1482

LOCATION	In Historic District, 1 block off Harrison Ave.
OPEN	All Year
DESCRIPTION	1875 Victorian Boarding House Eclectic furnishings
NO. OF ROOMS	2 w/private baths 4 w/shared baths
RATES	PB/$30-45 SB/$25-45 Reservation/cancellation policy
CREDIT CARDS	American Express
BREAKFAST	Full, served in dining room Dinner available w/advance notice Special diets accommodated
AMENITIES	Hot tub, fireplaces in some rooms, phone in sitting room, TV, books, games, musical instruments in parlor, kitchen, complimentary refreshments
RESTRICTIONS	No smoking. No pets (resident cats)
MEMBER	Homecomings

Wood Haven Manor

807 Spruce   PO Box 1291   Leadville, CO 80461   (719) 486-0109
Bobby & Jolene Wood, Resident Owners   *(800) 748-2570*

LOCATION	1-1/2 blocks west of Harrison Ave, right on Spruce, 2nd house on left
OPEN	All Year
DESCRIPTION	1899 Victorian Antique Victorian furnishings
NO. OF ROOMS	6 w/private baths 2 w/shared bath
RATES	PB/37-77 SB/$37-47 Reservation/cancellation policy Inquire about minimum stay during peak season
CREDIT CARDS	American Express, MasterCard, Visa
BREAKFAST	Full, served in dining room or guestrooms Special meals available
AMENITIES	Hot tub, robes in some rooms, TV/radio/phone in common area, complimentary refreshments
RESTRICTIONS	No smoking. No pets (resident dog)
RSO	B&B Rocky Mountains
MEMBER	B&B Innkeepers of Colorado Colorado Hotel & Lodging Assn.

LOVELAND

"Sweetheart City" is here, at the mouth of Big Thompson Canyon, 50 miles north of Denver via I-25 and Hwy. 34. Valentines are remailed from here w/Loveland's postmark and special cachet! This important agricultural and recreational area includes Boyd Lake State Recreational area, and some very good skiing at Loveland Ski Valley.

JEFFERSON HOUSE

342 E. 3rd St.   Loveland, CO 80537   (303) 669-6220
Art & Jeanne Myers, Resident Owners

LOCATION	Southeast corner of 3rd & Jefferson
OPEN	All Year
DESCRIPTION	1897 3-Story Brick Victorian Contemporary furnishings
NO. OF ROOMS	3 w/shared bath
RATES	$35-45
CREDIT CARDS	No
BREAKFAST	Continental, served in dining room
RESTRICTIONS	No smoking. No pets. No children

THE LOVELANDER
BED & BREAKFAST INN

217 W. 4th St.   Loveland, CO 80537   (303) 669-0798
Marilyn & Bob Wiltgen, Resident Owners

LOCATION	Center of town, just east of Garfield Ave. 5 mi. west of I-25
OPEN	All Year
DESCRIPTION	1902 Victorian Victorian furnishings
NO. OF ROOMS	9 w/private bath
RATES	$44-98 Reservation/cancellation policy
CREDIT CARDS	American Express, Discover, MasterCard, Visa
BREAKFAST	Full gourmet, served in dining room, garden or on veranda
AMENITIES	Radio in rooms, phone available, complimentary refreshments, separate meeting & special events center w/3-level deck, limited handicapped access, special gift & commemorative Valentine in February
RESTRICTIONS	No smoking. No pets. Children over 10
REVIEWED	*Colorado B&B Guide*
RSO	B&B Rocky Mountains
MEMBER	B&B Innkeepers of Colorado Distinctive Inns of Colorado Independent Innkeepers Assn. Professional Assn. of Innkeepers International
RATED	AAA 3 Diamonds

LYONS

A picturesque Western town, 45 miles northwest of Denver on Hwy. 36.

THE INN AT ROCK 'N RIVER: BED & BREAKFAST & TROUT FARM

16858 N. St. Vrain Dr.   PO Box 829   Lyons, CO 80540   (303) 443-4611
Ron & Imrie Anderson, Resident Owners   (800) 448-4611

LOCATION	3.2 mi. northwest of Lyons on Hwy. 36
OPEN	April 1-Nov. 29
DESCRIPTION	1950's-90's Scandinavian On 18 acres & the St. Vrain River Country furnishings
NO. OF ROOMS	8 w/private baths, king size beds & fully equipped kitchens
RATES	$55-65 Reservation/cancellation policy 2-night minimum on holiday weekends
CREDIT CARDS	American Express, Discover, MasterCard, Visa
BREAKFAST	Full, served in dining room, guestrooms or on patio Lunch & dinner available in restaurant
AMENITIES	Fishing in 2 stocked trout ponds, use of fishing rods & bait, cooking of catch, patio, waterfalls
RESTRICTIONS	Smoking restricted. No pets
RATED	AAA 2 Diamonds

MAHER

In the beautiful North Fork Valley of Gunnison country, 65 miles southwest of Grand Junction via Hwy. 50 and SR 92. The North Rim entrance to Black Canyon of the Gunnison National Monument, six miles north of Crawford.

CAMP STOOL RANCH BED & BREAKFAST

80367 Hwy. 92   PO Box 14   Maher, CO 81421   (303) 921-6461
George & Winnie Tracy, Resident Owners

LOCATION	6 mi. south of Crawford on Hwy. 92
OPEN	June-November
DESCRIPTION	1912 2-Story Rock House
NO. OF ROOMS	3 w/shared baths
RATES	Sgl/$30-35 Dbl/$40-50
CREDIT CARDS	No
BREAKFAST	Full or continental, served in dining area
RESTRICTIONS	None. Resident dogs
REVIEWED	*The Colorado Guide*

MANCOS

At the northeastern edge of Mesa Verde National Park, between Durango and Cortez via Hwys. 160 & 184.

TUCKER'S MOUNTAIN MEADOWS

37951 Hwy. 184   Mancos, CO 81328   (303) 533-7664
Keith & Sandra Tucker, Resident Owners

LOCATION	17 mi. east of Cortez off Hwy. 160
OPEN	All Year
DESCRIPTION	1974 Remodeled Classic Mountain Home Traditional furnishings
NO. OF ROOMS	4 w/private baths
RATES	$60-65 Reservation/cancellation policy
CREDIT CARDS	No
BREAKFAST	Full, served in dining room
AMENITIES	Complimentary refreshments
RESTRICTIONS	No smoking. No pets (Resident critters: dogs, cats, horses, llamas)
REVIEWED	*America's Wonderful Little Hotels & Inns* *Great Vacations with Your Kids*

Manitou Springs
(Colorado Springs)

The natural mineral waters once made this the gathering place for Ute & Arapaho Indian tribes. Now one of America's largest National Historic Districts, this small town with art colony overtones, is built on steep hillsides against the foothills of Pikes Peak.

The Barker House
Bed & Breakfast

819 Manitou Ave.   Manitou Springs, CO 80829   (719) 685-1400
Linda Sanden, Co-Manager   FAX: (719) 685-0179

LOCATION	Corner of Manitou Ave. & Navajo St.
OPEN	All Year
DESCRIPTION	1882 4-Story Gabled Victorian Eclectic furnishings National Historic Register Retirement Community
NO. OF ROOMS	4 w/private baths
RATES	$50-60 Reservation/cancellation policy Senior discounts
CREDIT CARDS	No
BREAKFAST	Continental plus, served in dining room Sunday brunch & dinners available
AMENITIES	Complimentary refreshments & ice cream socials, private entrances, landscaped courtyard
RESTRICTIONS	Smoking limited. No pets. Inquire about children

GRAY'S AVENUE HOTEL

711 Manitou Ave.   Manitou Springs, CO 80829   (719) 685-1277
Tom & Lee Gray, Resident Owners

LOCATION	Downtown on main street
OPEN	All Year
DESCRIPTION	1886 3-Story Queen Anne Shingled Victorian Antique furnishings
NO. OF ROOMS	3 w/private baths 7 w/shared baths
RATES	PB/$50-65 SB/$30-45 Reservation/cancellation policy
CREDIT CARDS	American Express, MasterCard, Visa
BREAKFAST	Full, served in dining room
AMENITIES	Radio in rooms, phone in lobby, fireplace in library, complimentary afternoon refreshments, small meeting facilities
RESTRICTIONS	No smoking. No pets (resident dog). Children 10 & over
REVIEWED	*The Colorado Guide* *Country Inns of the Rocky Mountain Region* *Country Inns, Lodges & Historic Hotels of the Midwest & Rocky Mountains* *The Old-House Lover's Guide to Inns and Bed & Breakfast Guest Houses*
RSO	B&B Rocky Mountains
MEMBER	B&B Innkeepers of Colorado

HISTORIC RED CRAGS BED & BREAKFAST

302 El Paso Blvd.   Manitou Springs, CO 80829   (719) 685-1920
Carrie & Kevin Maddox, Resident Owners

LOCATION	Corner of El Paso Blvd. & Rockledge
OPEN	All Year
DESCRIPTION	1870 Victorian Victorian furnishings National Historic Register
NO. OF ROOMS	6 w/private baths
RATES	$75-150 Reservation/cancellation policy
CREDIT CARDS	MasterCard, Visa
BREAKFAST	Full, served in dining room Catered dinners available
AMENITIES	Hot tub/sauna, robes, TV/radio/phone in rooms on request, fireplaces in rooms, meeting facilities, complimentary refreshments
RESTRICTIONS	No smoking. No pets (resident dogs). Children 13 & over
MEMBER	B&B Innkeepers of Colorado

ONALEDGE BED & BREAKFAST

336 El Paso Blvd.   Manitou Springs, CO 80829   (719) 685-4265
Shirley & Mel Podell, Resident Owners   *(800) 530-8253*

LOCATION	From Manitou Ave., 2 blocks west to Mayfair St. Right to El Paso Blvd., top of hill
OPEN	All Year
DESCRIPTION	1912 English Tudor Victorian furnishings
NO. OF ROOMS	2 w/private baths 2 suites w/private baths & hot tubs Reservation/cancellation policy
RATES	Rooms/$60-75 Suites/$95-120 Reservation/cancellation policy
CREDIT CARDS	American Express, Discover, MasterCard, Visa
BREAKFAST	Full gourmet, served in dining room or on patio
AMENITIES	TV/radio in rooms, fireplace in 1 room, complimentary refreshments, airport transportation
RESTRICTIONS	Smoking limited. No pets. Children limited
AWARDS	Top 50 Inns in the U.S., *INN Times*
REVIEWED	*Colorado B&B Guide* *Recommended Country Inns of the Rocky Mountain Region*
RSO	B&B Rocky Mountains
MEMBER	Colorado/Wyoming Lodging Assn. B&B Innkeepers of Colorado

Red Eagle Mountain
Bed & Breakfast Inn

616 Ruxton Ave.   Manitou Springs, CO 80829   (719) 685-4541
Stacie & Don LeVack, Resident Owners

LOCATION	West on Manitou Ave., left on Ruxton Ave., follow Cog Railway signs, 1 block past Cog Railway on right
OPEN	All Year
DESCRIPTION	1890 2-Story Queen Anne Victorian Antique & Victorian furnishings
NO. OF ROOMS	3 w/private baths
RATES	$60-75 Reservation/cancellation policy
CREDIT CARDS	MasterCard, Visa
BREAKFAST	Full, served in dining room, guestrooms or on 2nd-story balcony
AMENITIES	Radios in rooms, 1 room w/fireplace, 2nd story balcony w/gas grill, complimentary afternoon refreshments
RESTRICTIONS	None. Resident dogs & cat

RED STONE CASTLE

Manitou Springs, CO 80829   (719) 685-5070/5663
Greg McGrew & Cavan Daly-McGrew, Resident Owners

LOCATION	4-blocks from downtown, Manitou Ave. to Pawnee, to Southside Road, Castle gate
OPEN	All Year
DESCRIPTION	1892 Victorian Castle On 20 acres Antique & period furnishings National Historic Register
NO. OF ROOMS	2-room suite w/private bath & separate marble shower
RATES	Sgl/$95 Dbl/$120 Reservation/cancellation policy
CREDIT CARDS	No
BREAKFAST	Full, served in dining room or on patio
AMENITIES	Robes, TV/radio/phone, wet bar/refrigerator in suite, complimentary sherry, small reception & outdoor wedding facilities
RESTRICTIONS	No smoking. No pets (resident dog)
RSO	B&B Rocky Mountains

SUNNYMEDE BED & BREAKFAST

106 Spencer Ave. Manitou Springs, CO 80829 (719) 685-4619
Bill & Chris Power, Resident Owners (800) 553-5863

LOCATION	Residential neighborhood, on hill overlooking city. Cañon Ave. to Spencer Ave. (Cañon Ave. makes 90 degree turn in front of Post Office)
OPEN	All Year
DESCRIPTION	1885 Queen Anne Victorian
NO. OF ROOMS	1 w/private bath 2 w/shared bath
RATES	PB/$60 SB/$55-75 Reservation/cancellation policy
CREDIT CARDS	No
BREAKFAST	Full, served in dining room
AMENITIES	Robes, radio/phone in rooms, complimentary beverages
RESTRICTIONS	Smoking limited. No pets. Inquire about children
REVIEWED	*Christian B&B Directory*
RSO	B&B Rocky Mountains

TWO SISTERS INN

Ten Otoe Place   Manitou Springs, CO 80829   (719) 685-9684
Wendy Goldstein & Sharon Smith, Resident Owners

LOCATION	1 block from center of town & Historic District
OPEN	All Year
DESCRIPTION	1919 Victorian Bungalow Antique furnishings
NO. OF ROOMS	2 w/private baths 2 w/shared bath Separate cottage w/private bath
RATES	PB/$65 SB/$52 Cottage/$80 Reservation/cancellation policy
CREDIT CARDS	MasterCard, Visa
BREAKFAST	Full gourmet, served in dining room or garden Picnic lunches available w/advance notice
AMENITIES	Robes & fireplace in cottage, radio in rooms, TV/phone & fireplace in common room, private parking, complimentary refreshments
RESTRICTIONS	No smoking. No pets. Inquire about children
AWARDS	1990 Design Award, Overall Renovation, Historic Preservation Commission
RSO	B&B Rocky Mountains
MEMBER	National B&B Assn. B&B Innkeepers of Colorado Colorado Hotel and Motel Assn. Tourist House Assn. of America

MARBLE

The historical significance of this little community with a two-digit population, is the site of the famous Yule Marble Quarry. It's also only 7 miles southeast of delightful Redstone, on Hwy. 133 and CR 3.

THE INN AT RASPBERRY RIDGE

5580 County Rd. 3   Marble, CO 81623   (303) 963-3025
Gary & Patsy Wagner, Resident Owners

LOCATION	7 mi. southeast of Redstone
OPEN	All Year
DESCRIPTION	1960 Lodge
NO. OF ROOMS	5 w/private baths
RATES	$40-65
CREDIT CARDS	No
BREAKFAST	Full, served in dining room Other meals available on request
AMENITIES	TV/radio
RESTRICTIONS	No smoking. Inquire about pets

MESA

On the western edge of Grand Mesa, the world's largest flat top mountain and awesome natural wonder. East of Grand Junction via I-70 and SR 65.

TUTTLE RANCH BED & BREAKFAST

865 Hwy. 65   PO Box 244   Mesa, CO 81643   (303) 268-5869
Carolyn Tuttle, Resident Owner

LOCATION	On Grand Mesa, 3 mi. south of Mesa on Hwy. 65, 4 mi. north of Powderhorn Ski Resort
OPEN	All Year
DESCRIPTION	1978 Contemporary On 48 acre ranch
NO. OF ROOMS	4 w/shared bath
RATES	$30-35
CREDIT CARDS	No
BREAKFAST	Full, served in dining room
AMENITIES	Complimentary refreshments, trout pond & stream on property
RESTRICTIONS	No smoking. Resident dog & cat

MINTURN

A small pretty community 7 miles west of Vail, via I-70 Exit 171. It's a pleasant alternative to the spendy resort areas, and handy to the best of Vail Valley, and the Holy Cross & Eagles' Nest Wilderness Areas

THE EAGLE RIVER INN

145 N. Main   PO Box 100   Minturn CO 81645   (303) 827-5761
Beverly Rude, Manager   *(800) 344-1750*
Richard Galloway, Resident Owner   *FAX: (303) 827-4020*

LOCATION	Center of town
OPEN	All Year
DESCRIPTION	1894 Renovated Adobe Southwestern furnishings
NO. OF ROOMS	12 w/private baths
RATES	$79-190 Reservation/cancellation policy 3-night minimum on January-March weekends
CREDIT CARDS	American Express, MasterCard, Visa
BREAKFAST	Full, served in dining room
AMENITIES	Hot tub, TV/radio in rooms, complimentary evening wine & cheese, 2 sitting rooms, mountain bikes, small meeting facilities
RESTRICTIONS	No smoking. No pets (resident dog)
REVIEWED	*America's Wonderful Little Hotels and Inns* *B&B U.S.A.* *The Colorado Guide* *Country Inns & Back Roads* *Country Inns & Guesthouses* *Recommended Country Inns of the Rocky Mountain Region*
MEMBER	Colorado Hotel/Motel Assn. Distinctive Inns of Colorado
RATED	AAA 3 Diamonds Mobil 3 Stars

GAME CREEK BED & BREAKFAST

361 6th St.   Minturn, CO 81645   (303) 827-5839   FAX: (303) 476-6652
Mailing address: PO Box 4265   Vail, CO 81658
Oran & Paula Palmateer, Resident Owners

LOCATION	2 mi. south of Minturn I-70 Exit (map provided)
OPEN	Inquire
DESCRIPTION	1967 Split Level Contemporary & southwestern furnishings
NO. OF ROOMS	2 w/shared bath
RATES	$70-80
CREDIT CARDS	No
BREAKFAST	Full, served in dining room
AMENITIES	TV/radio/phone & fireplace in common area, refrigerator & laundry privileges
RESTRICTIONS	No smoking. No pets
RSO	B&B Vail/Ski Areas

MINTURN MEADOWS

321 6th Ave.   Minturn, CO 81620   (303) 827-5692
Mailing address: PO Box 2726   Avon, CO 81620
Virginia Dunlop, Resident Owner

LOCATION	In a cul-de-sac 1/2 mi. northeast of Minturn, over the bridge & railroad track
OPEN	All Year
DESCRIPTION	1920 Frame House Eclectic furnishings
NO. OF ROOMS	2 w/shared bath

RATES	Winter/$55-70 Summer/$40-50
	Reservation/cancellation policy
	2-night minimum
CREDIT CARDS	No
BREAKFAST	Winter/Full Summer/Continental
	Served in dining room
AMENITIES	TV in rooms, TV/VCR, books & magazines in living room, laundry facilities available, some kitchen privileges
RESTRICTIONS	Resident dog. Children over 12
RSO	B&B Vail/Ski Areas

TORTILLA FLAT

564 N. Taylor   Minturn, CO   (303) 827-4181
Mailing address: PO Box 1483   Vail, CO 81658
Mary & David Morgan, Resident Owners

LOCATION	In a cul-de-sac 1/2 mi. northeast of Minturn
OPEN	All Year
DESCRIPTION	1987 Rustic Ranch
	Antique oak furnishings
NO. OF ROOMS	1 suite w/private bath
RATES	$75-85
	Reservation/cancellation policy
	2-night minimum
CREDIT CARDS	No
BREAKFAST	Continental, served in suite
AMENITIES	Phone in suite, handicapped access
RESTRICTIONS	No smoking. No pets (resident cat). Inquire about children
RSO	B&B Vail/Ski Areas

Monte Vista

This is the agricultural trade center for the surrounding San Luis Valley, 17 miles west of Alamosa via Hwys. 285 & 160. Don't miss the Monte Vista National Wildlife Refuge for migratory birds, 6 miles east on Hwy. 15.

The Windmill Bed & Breakfast

4340 W. Hwy. 160   Monte Vista, CO 81144   (719) 852-0438
Evelyn & Bill Worker, Resident Owners

LOCATION	On Hwy. 160, 4 mi. west of junction of Hwys. 285 & 160
OPEN	All Year
DESCRIPTION	1960 Contemporary 1920's Era furnishings
NO. OF ROOMS	1 w/private bath 2 w/shared bath
RATES	PB/$30-40 SB/$40-50 Reservation/cancellation policy
CREDIT CARDS	No
BREAKFAST	Full, served in dining room Picnic lunches available
AMENITIES	Hot tub/sauna, complimentary refreshments
RESTRICTIONS	No smoking. No pets (resident dogs). Children over 6

MONTROSE

Gateway to Black Canyon of the Gunnison National Monument. This agricultural area at the junction of Hwy. 50 & 550, is rich in orchard crops and breathtaking landscapes.

FIFTH STREET BED & BREAKFAST

448 S. 5th   Montrose, CO 81401   (303) 249-4702
Norm & Dena Brooks, Resident Owners

LOCATION	5 blocks south of Townsend Ave., 2 blocks east on South 5th
OPEN	All Year
DESCRIPTION	1906 Victorian
NO. OF ROOMS	3 w/shared bath
RATES	$30-40 Reservation/cancellation policy
CREDIT CARDS	No
BREAKFAST	Full, served in dining room
AMENITIES	TV/radio/phone available on request, complimentary beverages
RESTRICTIONS	No smoking. No pets
RSO	B&B Rocky Mountains

Traveler's B&B Inn

502 S. 1st St.   Montrose, CO 81401   (303) 249-3472
Lois L. Hammans, Manager

LOCATION	2 blocks east of Hwy. 550, 1 block south of Hwy. 50
OPEN	All Year
DESCRIPTION	1910 2-Story Hotel
NO. OF ROOMS	8 w/private baths 7 w/shared bath
RATES	PB/$25-28 SB/$20-23 Reservation/cancellation policy
CREDIT CARDS	MasterCard, Visa
BREAKFAST	Full, served in dining room
AMENITIES	TV/radio in some rooms, complimentary beverages
RESTRICTIONS	No alcohol. Resident dog

Vee Broken Bracket

67255 Trout Rd.   Montrose, CO 81401   (303) 249-5609
Ralph & Ruby Woods, Resident Owners

LOCATION	6 mi. south of Montrose on Hwy. 550, 1/8 mi. east on Trout Rd.
OPEN	All Year
DESCRIPTION	1894 Red Brick Victorian Active farm/ranch operation
NO. OF ROOMS	3 w/shared baths
RATES	Sgl/$25-35 Dbl/$25-50 Reservation/cancellation policy
CREDIT CARDS	No
BREAKFAST	Continental plus, served in kitchen
AMENITIES	TV in 2 rooms, phone in hall
RESTRICTIONS	No smoking. Resident cat

MORRISON

A National Historic District and delightful little town just west of Denver, via I-70 and Hwy. 470, surrounded by incredible geological formations, including Red Rocks Park and Amphitheater. Near Soda Lakes and Bear Creek Reservoir.

CLIFF HOUSE LODGE BED & BREAKFAST INN & COTTAGES

Morrison Plaza   121 Stone St.   Morrison, CO 80465
Bari & Peggy Hahn, Resident Owners   (303) 697-9732

LOCATION	Center of town, 15 min. west of Denver
OPEN	All Year
DESCRIPTION	1873 Rose Sandstone French Antique furnishings National Historic Register
NO. OF ROOMS	2 w/private baths 2 w/shared bath 6 cabins w/private baths, 1 w/2 bedrooms Inquire about Honeymoon Suite
RATES	$49-149 Reservation/cancellation policy Weekly rates available
CREDIT CARDS	American Express
BREAKFAST	Full gourmet, served in dining room or on patio
AMENITIES	Hot tub, robes, TV/radio in rooms, fireplaces in some rooms, phone available, complimentary refreshments
RESTRICTIONS	Children & smoking in cabins only. No pets
REVIEWED	Recommended Country Inns of the Rocky Mountain Region

MOSCA

Just southwest of the Great Sand Dunes National Monument, about 15 miles north of Alamosa on Hwy. 17. Zapata Falls, 4 miles.

GREAT SAND DUNES
COUNTRY CLUB & INN

5303 Hwy. 150   Mosca, CO 81146   (719) 378-2357   (800) 284-9213
Hisayoti Ota, Owner   FAX: (719) 378-2428

LOCATION	4 mi. south of Great Sand Dunes National Monument on Hwy. 150
OPEN	April-November
DESCRIPTION	1880's Log Inn & Bunkhouse On working 100,000 acre Bison Ranch w/18-hole USGA Championship Golf Course
NO. OF ROOMS	15 w/private baths
RATES	$130-150
CREDIT CARDS	American Express, Discover, MasterCard, Visa
BREAKFAST	Continental plus, served in dining room Other meals available
AMENITIES	Complimentary health club facilities include: swimming pool/jacuzzi/sauna, exercise room. Fireplace in suite, TV, handicapped access, meeting facilities, mountain bikes & masseuse available at extra charge
RESTRICTIONS	No smoking. No pets

Norwood

A ranching community at the top of Wright's Mesa, near Miramonte Reservoir, 37 miles north of Telluride on Hwy. 145.

Back Narrows Inn & Restaurant

1550 Grand Ave.   PO Box 492   Norwood, CO 81423   (303) 327-4417
Richard & Nancy Parker, Resident Owners

LOCATION	Center of town
OPEN	All Year
DESCRIPTION	1890's Victorian
NO. OF ROOMS	2 w/private baths 11 w/shared baths
RATES	PB/$25-30 SB/$18-25
CREDIT CARDS	American Express, Diner's Club, MasterCard, Visa
BREAKFAST	Continental, served in dining room
	Dinner available in restaurant
AMENITIES	TV in 4 rooms

OHIO CITY

A miniscule community, and historic mining town in the Quartz Creek Valley, 24 miles northeast of Gunnison via Hwy. 50.

GOLD CREEK INN

8506 County Rd. 76   PO Box H-H   Ohio City, CO 81237
Joe Benge, Resident Owner   (303) 641-2086

LOCATION	12 mi. east of Gunnison on Hwy. 50 to Parlin. Turn left on Quartz Creek Rd. 12 mi. to Ohio City
OPEN	May-October
DESCRIPTION	1890 Hand-Hewn Log Antique furnishings
NO. OF ROOMS	2 w/shared bath
RATES	$39-49 Reservation/cancellation policy
CREDIT CARDS	MasterCard, Visa
BREAKFAST	Continental plus, served in dining room or guestrooms Dinner available Wed.-Sat.
AMENITIES	Fireplace in common area, deck, meeting facilities
RESTRICTIONS	No pets. Children over 12
REVIEWED	*The Colorado Guide* *Recommended Country Inns of the Rocky Mountain Region*

OURAY

This is visual magnificence at its finest that defies description. Situated in a natural mountain amphitheater, this mining town and National Historic District deserves to be called "The Switzerland of America." The drive from Montrose via Hwy. 550, The Million Dollar Highway, will leave you breathless. So will the many natural hot springs. Some of the best blue ice climbing in the country is here, too.

THE DAMN YANKEE BED & BREAKFAST INN

100 6th St.   PO Box 709   Ouray, CO 81427   *(800) 845-7512*
Joyce & Mike Manley, Resident Owners   *FAX: (303) 325-4912*

LOCATION	2 blocks from center of town on the Uncompahgre River
OPEN	All Year
DESCRIPTION	1990 European Cottage Antique Reproduction furnishings
NO. OF ROOMS	8 w/private bath
RATES	$58-145 Reservation/cancellation policy
CREDIT CARDS	MasterCard, Visa
BREAKFAST	Full gourmet, served in dining room
AMENITIES	Hot tub in gazebo, TV/phone in rooms, private entrances, down comforters, complimentary afternoon refreshments
RESTRICTIONS	No smoking. No pets. Children 12 & over
REVIEWED	*Best Places to Stay in the Rockies*
RSO	B&B Rocky Mountains
MEMBER	B&B Innkeepers of Colorado Distinctive Inns of Colorado Professional Assn. of Innkeepers International

KUNZ HOUSE BED & BREAKFAST

723 Fourth St.   PO Box 235   Ouray, CO 81427   (303) 325-4220
Sandy Kunz, Resident Owner

LOCATION	1 block east of Main St. in center of town
OPEN	All Year
DESCRIPTION	1898 2-Story Victorian Antique furnishings National Historic Register
NO. OF ROOMS	4 w/private baths 2 w/shared bath
RATES	$55-65
CREDIT CARDS	MasterCard, Visa
BREAKFAST	Full gourmet, served in dining room
AMENITIES	TV in living room, phone available, large porch, garden
RESTRICTIONS	No smoking. No pets. Inquire about children
REVIEWED	*Colorado B&B Guide* *Recommended Country Inns of the Rocky Mountain Region*

THE MANOR BED & BREAKFAST

317 Second St.   PO Box 80   Ouray, CO 81427   (303) 325-4574
Gem Mahan & Ivan Rudd, Innkeepers

LOCATION	1 block west of Main St. between 3rd & 4th Ave.
OPEN	All Year
DESCRIPTION	1890 3-Story Restored Victorian Antique furnishings National Historic Register
NO. OF ROOMS	7 w/private baths
RATES	Sgl/$45-55 Dbl/$55-70 Reservation/cancellation policy
CREDIT CARDS	MasterCard, Visa

BREAKFAST	Continental plus buffet, served in dining room
AMENITIES	Hot tub & deck, parlor w/fireplace & TV, morning room, phone in hall, croquet court, patio, balcony, complimentary afternoon refreshments, small meeting facilities
RESTRICTIONS	Smoking limited. No pets. Children 12 & over
REVIEWED	*Colorado B&B Guide* *Recommended Country Inns of the Rocky Mountain Region*
RSO	B&B Rocky Mountains
MEMBER	B&B Innkeepers of Colorado

OURAY 1898 HOUSE
BED & BREAKFAST

322 Main St.   PO Box 641   Ouray, CO 81427   (303) 325-4871
Lee & Kathy Bates, Resident Owners

LOCATION	Center of town
OPEN	May 30-Sept. 30
DESCRIPTION	1893 Renovated Victorian Victorian furnishings
NO. OF ROOMS	4 w/private baths
RATES	$38-68 Reservation/cancellation policy
CREDIT CARDS	MasterCard, Visa
BREAKFAST	Full, served in dining room
AMENITIES	TV in rooms, deck off each room, complimentary beverages
RESTRICTIONS	No smoking. No pets.
REVIEWED	*The Colorado Guide*
MEMBER	Tourist House Assn. of America

St. Elmo Hotel

426 Main St.   PO Box 667   Ouray, CO 81427   (303) 325-4951
Sandy & Dan Lingenfelter, Owners

LOCATION	Center of town
OPEN	All Year
DESCRIPTION	1898 Victorian Antique furnishings National Historic Register
NO. OF ROOMS	9 w/private baths
RATES	$58-84 Reservation/cancellation policy Minimum stay on some holidays
CREDIT CARDS	MasterCard, Visa
BREAKFAST	Full buffet, served in dining room Dinner available in restaurant
AMENITIES	Hot tub/sauna, parlour w/TV/books/games, complimentary refreshments, 1/2 price lift tickets for Telluride Ski Area, free pass to Ouray Hot Springs Pool
RESTRICTIONS	Smoking limited. No pets
REVIEWED	*America's Wonderful Little Hotels & Inns* *Colorado B&B Guide* *The Colorado Guide* *Recommended Country Inns of the Rocky Mountain Region*
RATED	AAA 2 Diamonds Mobil 3 Stars

WESTERN HOTEL BED & BREAKFAST

210 7th Ave.   PO Box 25   Ouray, CO 81427   (303) 325-4645
Tom & Tammy Kenning, Resident Owners

LOCATION	1/2 block west of Main St.
OPEN	All Year
DESCRIPTION	1891 Victorian Antique & period furnishings
NO. OF ROOMS	2 w/private baths 12 w/shared baths
RATES	PB/$68-78 SB/$42-50 Reservation/cancellation policy
CREDIT CARDS	MasterCard, Visa
BREAKFAST	Full, served in dining room Dinner available in restaurant
AMENITIES	Robes, meeting facilities
RESTRICTIONS	No smoking. No pets
REVIEWED	*The Colorado Guide* *Recommended Country Inns of the Rocky Mountain Region*
RSO	Ouray Central Reservations
MEMBER	B&B Innkeepers of Colorado

PAGOSA SPRINGS

This quiet, beautiful area surrounded by the San Juans, 60 miles east of Durango on Hwy. 160, sits on a hotbed of geothermal activity. Rainbow Hot Springs is definitely worth investigating. So is Echo Lake for fishing, and the incredible powder of Wolf Creek Ski Area 20 miles away.

DAVIDSON'S COUNTRY INN
BED & BREAKFAST

PO Box 87   Pagosa Springs, CO 81147   (303) 264-5863
Gilbert & Evelyn Davidson, Resident Owners

LOCATION	2 mi. east of Pagosa Springs on Hwy. 160
OPEN	All Year
DESCRIPTION	1980 3-Story Log On 32 acres Antique furnishings
NO. OF ROOMS	4 w/private bath 3 w/shared bath
RATES	PB/$42-62 SB/$38-44 Reservation/cancellation policy
CREDIT CARDS	MasterCard, Visa
BREAKFAST	Full, served in dining room
AMENITIES	Books/games/play corner in library, pool table and ping pong table in game room, fire pit, horseshoes, picnic table, sand box, complimentary afternoon refreshments
RESTRICTIONS	No smoking. Resident dog & cats
REVIEWED	*The Colorado Guide* *Recommended Country Inns of the Rocky Mountain Region*
MEMBER	B&B Innkeepers of Colorado Colorado Hotel and Motel Assn.

ROYAL PINE INN BED & BREAKFAST

4760 W. Hwy. 160   PO Box 4506   Pagosa Springs, CO 81157
Kathlyn Clare, Resident Owner   (800) 955-0274   (303) 731-4179

LOCATION	4 mi. west of town
OPEN	All Year
DESCRIPTION	1984 English Tudor w/Gift Shop Southwestern & Country furnishings
NO. OF ROOMS	3 w/private baths 2 w/shared bath
RATES	PB/$55 SB/$45 Reservation/cancellation policy Inquire about weekly rates & senior discount
CREDIT CARDS	MasterCard, Visa
BREAKFAST	Summer/Continental plus Winter/Full Served in dining room
AMENITIES	Robes, TV in rooms, complimentary refreshments, trips to hot springs, porta-crib, trailer parking, boarding of horses & various activities & excursions w/advance notice
RESTRICTIONS	No smoking. Inquire about pets
REVIEWED	*B&B in the U.S. & Canada* *Snowmobile Vacation Guide*
RSO	Pagosa Central Management
MEMBER	American Hotel and Motel Assn.

PAONIA

This fruit capitol of Colorado lies in the northern part of Black Canyon Country. Check out the Cherry Days Celebration on July 4. Also, Paonia Reservoir and State Recreation Area. From Glenwood Springs, south to Carbondale and southwest on Hwy. 133.

AGAPE INN

206 Rio Grande Ave.   PO Box 640   Paonia, CO 81428   (303) 527-4004
Jim & Norma Shutts, Resident Owners

LOCATION	Corner of 2nd & Rio Grande
OPEN	All Year
DESCRIPTION	1906 Victorian Country furnishings
NO. OF ROOMS	2 w/private baths 1 w/shared bath
RATES	$30-40 Reservation/cancellation policy
CREDIT CARDS	No
BREAKFAST	Full, served in dining room or breakfast nook
AMENITIES	TV in living room, complimentary refreshments
RESTRICTIONS	No smoking. No pets (resident dog). No alcohol
RSO	B&B Rocky Mountains

PARKER
(DENVER)

A residential country community, 25 miles southeast of Denver via I-25 Exit 193 (Lincoln Ave.). If you love country, check out the 3-day Parker Country Festival in June; the Horse & Carriage Driving Society Show in September; and the Christmas (Horse-pulled) Carriage Parade in December.

NOEL HOUSE BED & BREAKFAST INN

11020 S. Pikes Peak Dr.   Parker, CO 80134   (303) 841-8066
Penny Noel, Resident Owner

LOCATION	Parker Rd. south to Main St., east to S. Pikes Peak Dr., south to 11020
OPEN	All Year
DESCRIPTION	1910 Red School House Antique & country furnishings
NO. OF ROOMS	2 w/shared baths
RATES	$45 Reservation/cancellation policy
CREDIT CARDS	No
BREAKFAST	Full, served in dining room
AMENITIES	Hot tub/sauna, robes, radio in rooms, fireplace in breakfast room, complimentary evening dessert, meeting facilities
RESTRICTIONS	No smoking. No pets (resident cat & chickens). No children
RSO	B&B Rocky Mountains

PINE

This is a very small, wooded community southwest of Denver and 7 miles south of Conifer via Hwys. 285 and 67.

MEADOW CREEK BED & BREAKFAST INN

13438 Hwy. 285   Pine, CO 80470   (303) 838-4167/838-4899
Pat & Dennis Carnahan/Don & Judy Otis, Resident Owners

LOCATION	Take Hwy. 285 south from Denver. From the traffic light at Conifer, cont. 5.3 mi. Do not go down Elk Creek Rd. Our left is .2 mi. further. Turn, pass the school, take next left at Douglass Dr. at Douglass Ranch. Follow around to Berry Hill Lane. Turn right
OPEN	All Year
DESCRIPTION	1929 Mountain Stone On 35 acres Eclectic furnishings Colorado Historic Register
NO. OF ROOMS	6 w/private bath 1 cottage w/private bath
RATES	Rooms/$69-99 Cottage/$120 Reservation/cancellation policy Rooms/2-nights preferred Cottage/2-night minimum
CREDIT CARDS	MasterCard, Visa
BREAKFAST	Full, served in dining room, in guest room by special arrangement, or on deck Dinner available Wed.-Sat.
AMENITIES	Hot tub/sauna, fireplace in parlour & cottage, deck, gazebo, hammock, 1 rm. & cottage w/private jacuzzi, refrigerator/microwave in cottage, complimentary beverages & snacks, small meeting facilities
RESTRICTIONS	Smoking limited. No pets (resident dogs). Children under 12
AWARDS	1991 Top 50 Inns in America, *Inn Times*
RSO	B&B Rocky Mountains
MEMBER	B&B Innkeepers of Colorado Colorado/Wyoming Hotel Assn.

PUEBLO

The state's third largest city, 35 miles south of Colorado Springs, is home to the Colorado State Fair and the Pueblo Reservoir and State Recreation Area. Worth seeing is the Raptor Rehabilitation Center and Nature Center.

ABRIENDO INN

300 W. Abriendo Ave.   Pueblo, CO 81004   (719) 544-2703
Kerrelyn & Chuck Trent, Resident Owners

LOCATION	I-25 Exit 97B. Right on Abriendo Ave. to corner of Jackson St.
OPEN	All Year
DESCRIPTION	1906 Four Square Classical Antique furnishings National Historic Register
NO. OF ROOMS	7 w/private baths
RATES	$49-89 Reservation/cancellation policy
CREDIT CARDS	American Express, Diner's Club, MasterCard, Visa
BREAKFAST	Full, served in dining room or on porch
AMENITIES	TV/radio/phones in rooms, parlor, park-like grounds, complimentary evening refreshments, small meeting facilities
RESTRICTIONS	No smoking. No pets. Children 7 & over
RSO	B&B Rocky Mountains
MEMBER	Distinctive Inns of Colorado B&B Innkeepers of Colorado

RED CLIFF

This little mining town 15 miles south of Vail off I-70 is famous for its location at the base of Shrine Pass, and its view of Mt. of the Holy Cross. This is also the trail head for the Tenth Mountain Trail Association Hut System.

THE PILGRIM'S INN

101 Eagle St.   PO Box 151   Red Cliff, CO 81649   (303) 827-5333
Michael Wasmer, Resident Owner   *FAX: (303) 827-5395*

LOCATION	Center of town, on Turkey Creek
OPEN	All Year
DESCRIPTION	1905 Victorian
NO. OF ROOMS	2 w/private baths 2 w/shared bath
RATES	PB/$65-85 SB/$60-70 Reservation/cancellation policy 2-night minimum during Christmas, Feb. & March
CREDIT CARDS	MasterCard, Visa
BREAKFAST	Full, served in dining area
AMENITIES	Hot tub, complimentary refreshments, small meeting facilities
RESTRICTIONS	No smoking
RSO	B&B Rocky Mountains
MEMBER	B&B Innkeepers of Colorado

PLUM HOUSE BED & BREAKFAST

236 Eagle St.   PO Box 41   Red Cliff, CO 81649   (303) 827-5881
Sydney Summers, Resident Owner

LOCATION	Middle of town, look for plum house
OPEN	All Year
DESCRIPTION	1940's House Antique furnishings
NO. OF ROOMS	1 w/shared 1-1/2 bath
RATES	$50-60
CREDIT CARDS	No
BREAKFAST	Full, served in kitchen Dinner available w/24 hr. notice
AMENITIES	Hot tub, down comforter & pillows, wood stove, TV/VCR/radio/stereo, music & books in living room, complimentary refreshments on request
RESTRICTIONS	No smoking. No pets. No children

REDSTONE

The famous Redstone Castle illustrates the historic spirit of this arty, pleasantly-odd Victorian coal-mining town, 30 miles south of Glenwood Springs, via Hwy. 82 & 133.

AVALANCHE RANCH

12863 Hwy. 133   Redstone, CO 81623   (303) 963-2846
Jim & Sharon Mollica, Resident Owners

LOCATION	5 mi. north of Redstone
OPEN	All Year
DESCRIPTION	1913 Farmhouse w/cabins, antique shop & restaurant On 45 acres on Crystal River Country furnishings
NO. OF ROOMS	Main house: 2 w/private bath 2 w/shared bath 11 cabins w/private baths & kitchens
RATES	Rooms/PB/$90 SB/$75-80 Cabins/$75-110 Reservation/cancellation policy 2-night minimum on summer weekends & holidays
CREDIT CARDS	Discover, MasterCard, Visa
BREAKFAST	Continental, served in dining room or guestrooms on request Other meals available for special events
AMENITIES	Robes, sitting & dining rooms w/fireplaces, tree house, tire swing, play room, gift shop, wedding/reception/meeting facilities
RESTRICTIONS	No smoking. No pets (resident dog, cat, farm animals)
REVIEWED	*The Colorado B&B Guide*
RSO	B&B Rocky Mountains Glenwood Central Reservations Off the Beaten Path
MEMBER	B&B Innkeepers of Colorado Colorado Campground and CabinResort Assn. Professional Assn. of Innkeepers International

CLEVEHOLM MANOR
(THE HISTORIC REDSTONE CASTLE)

0058 Redstone Blvd.   Redstone, CO 81623   (303) 963-3463
Cyd Lange, Manager   *(800) 643-4837*

LOCATION	1 mi. south of Redstone
OPEN	All Year
DESCRIPTION	1902 English Tudor Manor National Historic Register
NO. OF ROOMS	8 w/private baths 8 w/shared bath
RATES	PB/$110-167 SB/$78 Reservation/cancellation policy
CREDIT CARDS	American Express, MasterCard, Visa
BREAKFAST	Continental, served in dining room Dinner available on Fri. & Sat.
AMENITIES	Robes, down comforters, fireplaces in rooms, game room, lawn games, complimentary refreshments
RESTRICTIONS	No smoking. No pets (resident dog). No children
REVIEWED	*America's Wonderful Little Hotels & Inns* *Colorado B&B Guide* *The Colorado Guide* *Recommended Country Inns of the Rocky Mountain Region*
MEMBER	Distinctive Inns of Colorado Colorado Hotel and Motel Assn.

RIDGWAY

This very western ranching community in the San Juan Mountains, 10 miles north of Ouray on Hwy. 550, was the filming location for "True Grit" and "How the West Was Won." (Try a "Duke" sandwich at the True Grit Cafe!)

THE ADOBE INN

---

251 Liddell Dr.   PO Box 470   Ridgway, CO 81432-0470   (303) 626-5939
Terre & Joyce Bucknam, Resident Owners

LOCATION	1 block south of Hwy. 62
OPEN	All Year
DESCRIPTION	1984 Adobe Country Inn w/Mexican Restaurant
NO. OF ROOMS	3 w/shared baths 8-bed dorm also available
RATES	Rooms/$35-40 Dorm/$12 Reservations recommended
CREDIT CARDS	American Express, MasterCard, Visa
BREAKFAST	Continental, served in dining room Dinner available in restaurant
AMENITIES	TV/radio in rooms, fireplace in dining room, phone in hallway, passive solar heat
RESTRICTIONS	None. Resident cat
REVIEWED	*The Colorado Guide* *Recommended Country Inns of the Rocky Mountain Region*

SALIDA

On the banks of the Arkansas River, this is the jumping-off place for whitewater rafting. Check out the hot springs pool and downtown Historic District, 117 miles southwest of Denver on Hwy. 285.

THE POOR FARM COUNTRY INN

8495 County Rd. 160   Salida, CO 81201   (719) 539-3818
Herb & Dottie Hostetler, Resident Owners

LOCATION	3 mi. east of Hwy. 285 off County Rd. 160
OPEN	All Year
DESCRIPTION	1892 2-Story Stone Victorian Antique furnishings National Historic Register
NO. OF ROOMS	2 w/private baths 3 w/shared bath Coed dorm w/12 beds
RATES	PB/$51 SB/$41 Dorm/$20 Reservation/cancellation policy
CREDIT CARDS	MasterCard, Visa
BREAKFAST	Full, served in dining room
AMENITIES	Library, complimentary beverages, private fishing in Arkansas River
RESTRICTIONS	Smoking limited. No pets (resident dogs & cats)
REVIEWED	*America's Wonderful Little Hotels & Inns* *Best Bed & Breakfasts & Country Inns: West* *Colorado B&B Guide* *The Colorado Guide* *Motorcycle B&B* *Recommended Country Inns of the Rocky Mountain Region*
RSO	B&B Rocky Mountains
MEMBER	B&B Innkeepers of Colorado

San Luis

Here in the sportsman's paradise of the San Luis Valley, the oldest town in Colorado is still built around its adobe plaza, 50 miles south of Fort Garland on Hwy. 59.

El Convento Bed & Breakfast

512 Church Place   PO Box 326   San Luis, CO 81152   (719) 672-4223
Owned by Sangre de Cristo Parish, Father Patrick Valdez, Exec. Dir.
Laurie TenPas, Resident Manager

LOCATION	2 blocks west of Main St., across from Catholic Church
OPEN	All Year
DESCRIPTION	1905 2-Story Adobe Convent Southwestern furnishings
NO. OF ROOMS	4 w/private baths
RATES	$40-50 Reservation/cancellation policy
CREDIT CARDS	MasterCard, Visa
BREAKFAST	Full gourmet, served in dining room
AMENITIES	Library, art gallery, small meeting room
RESTRICTIONS	$25 deposit for pets (resident dog)
REVIEWED	*The Colorado Guide*
RSO	B&B Rocky Mountains

SILVER PLUME

This old mining camp, 48 miles west of Denver on I-70 is part of the Georgetown-Silver Plume National Historic District. Take a ride on the historic Georgetown Loop Railroad, and scan the rocky cliffs for Bighorn Sheep.

BREWERY INN BED & BREAKFAST

246 Main St.   PO Box 473   Silver Plume, CO 80476-0473
Robin Boone, Manager   (303) 674-5565

LOCATION	I-70 Exit 226, turn right, then left on Main, 3rd house on left
OPEN	All Year
DESCRIPTION	1857 2-Story Victorian
NO. OF ROOMS	6 w/private baths 3 w/shared bath
RATES	PB/$40-60 SB/$35-40 Reservation/cancellation policy
CREDIT CARDS	MasterCard, Visa
BREAKFAST	Continental plus, served in kitchen
AMENITIES	Fireplaces in rooms, complimentary beverages, meeting facilities, handicapped access, gazebo
RESTRICTIONS	No pets
REVIEWED	*The Colorado Guide*
RSO	B&B Rocky Mountains

SILVERTHORNE
(SUMMIT COUNTY)

Tucked at the base of Buffalo Peak in the Lake Dillon area, 70 miles west of Denver, the gold medal Blue River winds through town, and there's good putting on the Eagle's Nest Golf Course. Check out the Factory Discount Outlet Mall.

GORE RANGE BED & BREAKFAST

PO Box 286   396 Tanglewood Ln.   Silverthorne, CO 80498
Jim & Edna Parham, Resident Owners   (303) 468-5786

LOCATION	2 blocks north of I-70 Exit 205 on Ptarmigan Mt.
OPEN	All Year
DESCRIPTION	1973 Contemporary 2-Story Cedar Contemporary furnishings
NO. OF ROOMS	1 w/private bath 2 w/shared bath 1 suite w/private bath & fireplace
RATES	PB/$40-65 SB/$35-70 Suite/$80-130 Reservation/cancellation policy
CREDIT CARDS	No
BREAKFAST	Full, served in dining room
AMENITIES	TV/radio/phones in rooms, TV/VCR & fireplace in living room, complimentary refreshments, refrigerator & laundry facilities
RESTRICTIONS	No smoking. No pets. No children
RSO	B&B Rocky Mountains
MEMBER	Summit County B&B Assn.

MOUNTAIN VISTA BED & BREAKFAST

PO Box 1398   358 Lagoon Ln.   Silverthorne, CO 80498   (303) 468-7700
Bob & Sandy Ruggaber, Resident Owners   (800) 333-5165

LOCATION	I-70 Exit 205 north onto Hwy. 9, turn right at Wendy's onto Tanglewood Ln, left at Lagoon Ln.
OPEN	All Year
DESCRIPTION	1976 2-Story Contemporary Contemporary furnishings
NO. OF ROOMS	1 w/private bath 2 w/shared bath
RATES	$50-75 Reservation/cancellation policy
CREDIT CARDS	No
BREAKFAST	Full, served in dining room
AMENITIES	Robes, radio in rooms, TV, games, books, puzzles, & fireplace in living rooms, guest kitchen, ski & bike storage, complimentary refreshments, outdoor grill
RESTRICTIONS	No pets (resident dog). Children under 6
MEMBER	Summit County B&B Assn.

Puddin' and the Fat Cat

Through Reservation Service Only:
PO Box 491   Vail, CO 81658   (303) 949-1212   (800) 748-2666

LOCATION •	5 min. from center of town
OPEN	All Year
DESCRIPTION	1980 Contemporary w/vaulted ceilings
NO. OF ROOMS	1 w/private bath
RATES	$40-75 Reservation/cancellation policy
CREDIT CARDS	MasterCard, Visa
BREAKFAST	Full, served in dining room or guestroom
AMENITIES	TV/radio/phone in rooms, complimentary refreshments
RESTRICTIONS	No smoking. No pets (resident cats). No children
RSO	B&B Assn. of Vail/Ski Areas

SILVERTON

This National Historic Landmark, on the new San Juan Skyway, is ornate Victorian at its grandest. In the incomparable setting of the San Juan, Rio Grande and Uncompahgre National Forests, the Durango & Silverton Narrow Gauge Railroad terminates here, 45 miles north of Durango on Hwy. 550.

ALMA HOUSE HOTEL

220 E. 10th St.   PO Box 359   Silverton, CO 81433   (303) 387-5336
Christine Payne, Resident Owner

LOCATION	1 block off Main St.
OPEN	All Year
DESCRIPTION	1896 2-Story Western Victorian Furnishings
NO. OF ROOMS	3 suites w/private baths 8 w/shared baths
RATES	PB/$70 SB/$35-38
CREDIT CARDS	American Express, MasterCard, Visa
BREAKFAST	Continental, served in dining room or guestrooms Lunch, dinner & room service available
AMENITIES	TV/radio in rooms, complimentary coffee
RESTRICTIONS	No smoking. Resident dogs

CHRISTOPHER HOUSE BED & BREAKFAST

821 Empire St.   PO Box 241   Silverton, CO 81433   (303) 387-5857
Eileen Swonger, Resident Owner   Oct.-May: (904) 567-7549

LOCATION	4 blocks from train depot & business district
OPEN	June-Sept.
DESCRIPTION	1894 Victorian Victorian furnishings National Historic Register
NO. OF ROOMS	2 w/private baths 3 w/shared bath
RATES	PB/$42-52 SB/$32-42 Reservation/cancellation policy
CREDIT CARDS	No
BREAKFAST	Full, served in dining room
AMENITIES	TV in 1 room, guest parlor w/cable TV & fireplace, complimentary refreshments, small meeting facilities, limited handicapped access
RESTRICTIONS	No smoking. No pets
REVIEWED	B&B U.S.A. Christian B&B Guide

SMEDLEYS BED & BREAKFAST

1314 Greene St.   PO Box 2   Silverton, CO 81433   (303) 387-5423
Fritz Klinke & Loren Lew, Owners/Managers   (800) 342-4338

LOCATION	Center of town, above Smedleys Ice Cream Parlor, next door to The Pickle Barrel Restaurant
OPEN	All Year
DESCRIPTION	1979 Victorian Victorian & contemporary furnishings

226

NO. OF ROOMS	3 suites w/private baths, kitchens & living rooms
RATES	Sgl/$36 Dbl/$47 15% discount for 4 + days Reservation/cancellation policy
CREDIT CARDS	American Express, Diner's Club, Discover, Encore, MasterCard, Visa
BREAKFAST	Full, served in adjacent French Bakery Other meals available in restaurant
AMENITIES	TV/HBO in suites, complimentary beverages, meeting facilities available at French Bakery
RESTRICTIONS	No pets
REVIEWED	*Recommended Country Inns of the Rocky Mountain Region*

TELLER HOUSE HOTEL

1250 Greene St.   PO Box 2   Silverton, CO 81433   (303) 387-5423
Fritz Klinke & Loren Lew, Owners/Managers   (800) 342-4338

LOCATION	Center of town, above The French Bakery Restaurant
OPEN	All Year
DESCRIPTION	1896 Restored Victorian
NO. OF ROOMS	2 w/private baths 5 w/shared baths
RATES	PB/$35-45 SB/$23-29 Reservation/cancellation policy Affiliated w/American Youth Hostels
CREDIT CARDS	American Express, Diner's Club, Discover, Encore, MasterCard, Visa
BREAKFAST	Full, served downstairs in The French Bakery
AMENITIES	Meeting facilities
RESTRICTIONS	No pets

WINGATE HOUSE BED & BREAKFAST

1045 Snowden St.   PO Box 2   Silverton, CO 81433   *(303) 387-5423*
Fritz Klinke & Loren Lew, Owners/Managers   *(800) 342-4338*

LOCATION	2 blocks from center of town
OPEN	All Year
DESCRIPTION	1886 Victorian
NO. OF ROOMS	3 w/shared baths 1 suite w/shared baths
RATES	$35-45 Reservation/cancellation policy Special occasion rates on request
CREDIT CARDS	American Express, Diner's Club, Discover, Encore, MasterCard, Visa
BREAKFAST	Full, served at French Bakery Restaurant
AMENITIES	TV/HBO in living room, phone available, guest kitchen, complimentary beverages, meeting facilities at French Bakery
RESTRICTIONS	No pets. No smoking
REVIEWED	*The Colorado Guide* *Recommended Country Inns of the Rocky Mountain Region*

SNOWMASS
(ASPEN)

Part of the Aspen complex, but just far enough away from the glitz, pristine and tranquil skiing is what Snowmass is all about. It's highly-rated for its ski schools and family programs, and there is ski-in and ski-out everything. 28 miles southeast of Glenwood Springs and 12 miles from Aspen via Hwy. 82.

ASPEN HOUSE

---

908 Wood Rd. PO Box 5274 Snowmass Village, CO 81615
Fred K. Gamble, Resident Manager (303) 923-4300

LOCATION	On Ski Lift 7 (Funnel Lift), 200 yds. directly across from center of Snowmass Village Mall
OPEN	Thanksgiving-October
DESCRIPTION	1978 Wood Mansion Contemporary furnishings
NO. OF ROOMS	4 master suites w/private whirlpool baths, sauna, sitting room, fireplace, TV/VCR
RATES	$300-600 Reservation/cancellation policy
CREDIT CARDS	No
BREAKFAST	Full, served in dining room Dinner available at extra charge
AMENITIES	Therapy Room w/10-person hot tub, sauna & exercise equipment, robes, natural swimming pond/waterfall, tennis court, ping pong room, multi-level sundeck, generous apres-ski buffet & summer refreshments, complimentary bar, large screen TV/VCR & cassettes, complimentary airport pickup & use of house vehicles (mileage charge during non-ski season), conference room facilities, 24-hour staff on premises
RESTRICTIONS	No smoking. No pets. No children

CONNABLES' GUEST HOME

3747 Brush Creek Rd.   PO Box 5380   Snowmass Village, CO 81615
CeCe & Bruce Connable, Resident Owners   (303) 923-5034

LOCATION	1/2 mi. from Snowmass Ski Resort & directly across from Snowmass Club Golf Course
OPEN	Thanksgiving to Mid-April & Mid-June to Mid-Sept.
DESCRIPTION	1991 Renovated Contemporary Wood & Log Eclectic & southwestern furnishings
NO. OF ROOMS	1 w/private bath 2 w/shared bath
RATES	Winter: Sgl(Queen/twin)/$85 Dbl(King/queen/twin)/$125-145 Christmas/$125-145 Inquire about summer rates Reservation/cancellation policy
CREDIT CARDS	No
BREAKFAST	Full gourmet, served in dining room or kitchen island
AMENITIES	Hot tub/sauna, robes, deck, TV/radio & fireplaces in den & living room, fireplace in dining room, phone available, complimentary summer refreshments/hor d'oeuvres & winter aprés ski, complimentary family barbeque for weekly guests
RESTRICTIONS	No smoking. No pets (resident cat)

Snowmass Village Bed & Breakfast

686 Oakridge Rd.   PO Box 5446   Snowmass Village, CO 81615
Grace Oliphant, Resident Owner   (303) 923-3649

LOCATION	On side of a mountain 2 mi. from Snowmass Village
OPEN	All Year
DESCRIPTION	1970 Cedar & Shake On 5 acres Antique & country furnishings
NO. OF ROOMS	2 w/private baths
RATES	Inquire about rates Reservation/cancellation policy 2-night minimum
CREDIT CARDS	No
BREAKFAST	Continental or continental plus, served in dining room Special meals available
AMENITIES	TV/radio/phone/fireplaces in rooms, complimentary refreshments
RESTRICTIONS	No smoking. No children. Resident dogs

STARRY PINES

2262 Snowmass Creek Rd.   Snowmass, CO 81654   (303) 927-4202
Shelley Burke, Resident Owner

LOCATION	2 mi. west of Snowmass from Hwy. 82 (Conoco Station)
OPEN	All year
DESCRIPTION	1982 Contemporary Stone & White Ash On 70 acres
NO. OF ROOMS	2 w/private 1/2 baths & shared shower 1 apartment w/private bath, refrigerator & sink alcove, deck
RATES	Rooms/$80-90 Apartment/$100-120 Reservation/cancellation policy 2-night minimum during ski season
CREDIT CARDS	No
BREAKFAST	Continental plus, served in dining room or on balcony overlooking stream
AMENITIES	Hot tub, fireplace & satellite TV in living room, complimentary refreshments, horse boarding facilities on property
RESTRICTIONS	No smoking. No pets (resident cat). Children over 6
RSO	B&B Rocky Mountains

STEAMBOAT SPRINGS

This "Ski Town USA" is a world class resort and cowboy-populated ranching area that bubbles with 157 natural hot springs. The week-long Winter Carnival in February and summer rodeos are worth the trip. Check out spectacular Fish Creek Falls. 166 miles northwest of Denver via I-70 and Hwy. 40.

CLERMONT INN

917 Lincoln Ave.   PO Box 774927   Steamboat Springs, CO 80477
Mark & Mimi Witcher, Resident Owners   (303) 879-3083

LOCATION	Center of town, between 9th & 10th Sts.
OPEN	Nov. 20-April 12 & June 5-Oct. 25
DESCRIPTION	1942 Victorian Motor Inn
NO. OF ROOMS	22 w/private 1/2 baths & shared tub/showers
RATES	Summer/Per Room/$40-50 2 Room Units/$60-80 Winter/Per Room/$50-100 2 Room Units/$100-190
CREDIT CARDS	MasterCard, Visa
BREAKFAST	Full, served in dining room
AMENITIES	Hot tub in game room, fireplace in library, TV in rooms, ski lockers, free bus pass, meeting facilities, handicapped access, off-street parking
RESTRICTIONS	None
REVIEWED	*The Colorado Guide*
RSO	B&B Rocky Mountains

CRAWFORD HOUSE

1184 Crawford Ave.   PO Box 775062   Steamboat Springs, CO 80477
Jerry & Pam Nettleton, Resident Owners   (303) 879-1859

LOCATION	Center of town, 4 mi. from ski area
OPEN	All Year
DESCRIPTION	1894 3-Story Victorian Antique furnishings
NO. OF ROOMS	1 w/private bath 1 w/shared bath
RATES	PB/$60-75 SB/$55-65 Reservation/cancellation policy
CREDIT CARDS	No
BREAKFAST	Continental plus, served in dining room or guestrooms
AMENITIES	Hot tub/sauna, parlor w/TV/stereo & fireplace, complimentary late night snack & turn down service
RESTRICTIONS	No smoking. No pets (resident dog)
MEMBER	B&B Innkeepers of Colorado

ELK RIVER ESTATES

Box 5032   Steamboat Springs, CO 80477-5032   (303) 879-7556
Bill Fetcher, Resident Owner

LOCATION	5 mi. northwest of Steamboat Springs, on County Rd. 129
OPEN	All Year
DESCRIPTION	B&B Host Home. 1973 ranch
NO. OF ROOMS	1 W/private bath
RATES	$35-40
CREDIT CARDS	No
BREAKFAST	Full, served in kitchen Other meals by request
AMENITIES	TV/radio, complimentary refreshments
RESTRICTIONS	No smoking. No pets (resident cat). No children

234

GRAND HOUSE BED & BREAKFAST

724 Grand St.   PO Box 771311   Steamboat Springs, CO 80477
Karen & Chris Klemz, Resident Owners   (303) 879-1939

LOCATION	7 blocks from historic Old Town, 1/2 block from ski shuttle
OPEN	All Year
DESCRIPTION	1985 Contemporary Contemporary furnishings
NO. OF ROOMS	1 w/private bath 2 w/shared bath
RATES	PB/$50-85 SB/$40-70 Reservation/cancellation policy 2-night minimum during ski season
CREDIT CARDS	No
BREAKFAST	Continental plus, served in Hearth Room Special meals available on request
AMENITIES	TV/radio/phone/fireplace in suite, guest kitchen, laundry facilities
RESTRICTIONS	No smoking. No pets (resident dog)

HIGH MEADOWS RANCH

20505 RCR #16   Oak Creek, CO 80467   (800) 457-4453   (303) 736-8416
Mailing address: PO Box 771216 Steamboat Springs, CO 80477
Dennis & Jan Stamp, Resident Owners

LOCATION	7.5 mi. south of Stagecoach State Reservoir, on Rutt County Rd. #16, 25 mi. south of Steamboat Springs
OPEN	All Year
DESCRIPTION	1989 & 1991 Contemporary Log Chalets Western & southwestern furnishings
NO. OF ROOMS	5 w/private baths
RATES	$50-75 Inquire about 3 & 5 day all-inclusive packages & whole chalet rates Reservation/cancellation policy
CREDIT CARDS	MasterCard, Visa
BREAKFAST	Full, served in dining room Lunch, dinner & special meals available
AMENITIES	Hot tub/sauna, complete kitchens, laundry & small meeting facilities, handicapped access. Guided or drop trips for cross-country skiing & the back country, horseback riding available, barbeques & steak rides, airport transportation arranged
RESTRICTIONS	None. Resident dog, cats & horses

OAK STREET BED & BREAKFAST

702 Oak St.   PO Box 772434   Steamboat Springs, CO 80477
Jill & Seth Coit, Resident Owners   (303) 870-0484   FAX: (303) 870-0484

LOCATION	Center of town, corner of Oak & 7th Sts.
OPEN	All Year
DESCRIPTION	1930 Victorian House w/Private Guest Cottages Antique furnishings

NO. OF ROOMS	10 w/private baths 2 w/shared bath
RATES	Summer/$40-60 Winter/$60-110
	Reservation/cancellation policy
CREDIT CARDS	MasterCard, Visa
BREAKFAST	Full gourmet, served in dining area
AMENITIES	Hot tub/sauna, robes, TV/VCR in rooms, phone available, complimentary coffee, meeting facilities
RESTRICTIONS	Smoking limited. No pets. Children over 6

SCANDINAVIAN LODGE

2883 Burgess Creek Rd.   PO Box 774484   Steamboat Springs, CO 84077
(303) 879-0517   (800) 233-8102   FAX: (303) 879-0943
Margareta Olsson, Resident Owner

LOCATION	At the Thunderhead lift, 1-1/2 mi. northeast of Village Circle, 1/2 way up the lower mountain
OPEN	May 15-April 20
DESCRIPTION	1973 Swedish Lodge & Restaurant
	Swedish furnishings
NO. OF ROOMS	26 w/private baths
RATES	$39-109
	Reservation/cancellation policy
	Inquire about minimum stays
CREDIT CARDS	No
BREAKFAST	Full buffet, served in dining room
	Lunch & dinner available in restaurant
AMENITIES	Swimming pool, hot tub/sauna, tennis courts, volleyball net, TV in rooms, phone in some rooms, meeting facilities
RESTRICTIONS	No smoking
REVIEWED	*Great Ski Inns & Hotels of America*

STEAMBOAT BED & BREAKFAST

442 Pine St.   PO Box 772058   Steamboat Springs, CO 80477
Stephen Evans, Resident Owner   (303) 879-5724

LOCATION	2 blocks north of Main St.
OPEN	All Year
DESCRIPTION	1889 2-Story Victorian Antique Victorian furnishings
NO. OF ROOMS	5 w/private baths
RATES	$60-80 Reservation/cancellation policy
CREDIT CARDS	MasterCard, Visa
BREAKFAST	Full, served in dining room
AMENITIES	Complimentary fruit & beverages, Music Conservatory w/TV & movies, deck, airport transportation available
RESTRICTIONS	No smoking. No pets. No children
RSO	B&B Rocky Mountains

STERLING

Located on the South Platte River in the extreme northeast corner of Colorado, it is a straight shot between Denver and Ogallala, Nebraska on I-76, and a major trade center for the area's agricultural operations. Check out its famous "Living Tree Sculptures" and nearby Sterling Reservoir and Pawnee National Grasslands.

THE CREST HOUSE BED & BREAKFAST

516 S. Division Ave. Sterling, CO 80751 (303) 522-3753
Julius & Barbara Rico, Resident Owners

LOCATION	Near center of town, corner of Division & Denver
OPEN	All Year
DESCRIPTION	1912 3-Story Victorian Victorian furnishings
NO. OF ROOMS	1 w/private bath 4 w/shared baths
RATES	PB/$40-50 SB/$35-45
CREDIT CARDS	MasterCard, Visa
BREAKFAST	Full, served in dining room Other meals available by request
AMENITIES	TV/HBO, phone & fireplaces in rooms, complimentary late night snacks & coffee, Sunday Brunch, meeting facilities
RESTRICTIONS	No smoking. No pets (resident parrot)
MEMBER	B&B Innkeepers of Colorado

TELLURIDE

This is a tiny Victorian gem set in a box canyon high in the San Juan Mountains. It's famous for its skiing and proliferation of nationally-known summer events, including its jazz, bluegrass, film, and hang-gliding festivals. 300 miles southwest of Denver via US 285, 50, Hwy. 62 & 145.

ALPINE INN BED & BREAKFAST

PO Box 2398   440 W. Colorado   Telluride, CO 81435   (303) 728-6282
The Weaner Family, Resident Owners

LOCATION	Center of town near ski lifts
OPEN	Thanksgiving-May 1 & June 1-October 15
DESCRIPTION	1907 Restored Victorian Antique furnishings National Historic Register
NO. OF ROOMS	2 w/private baths 2 w/shared bath
RATES	Summer (Non-festival)/$65-100 Winter/Inquire Reservation/cancellation policy
CREDIT CARDS	American Express, MasterCard, Visa
BREAKFAST	Full, served in dining room
AMENITIES	Solarium w/jaccuzi & 280-degree view of valley & mountains, off street parking
RESTRICTIONS	No smoking. No children
REVIEWED	*Colorado B&B Guide*
RSO	Tulluride Central Reservations

Bear Creek Bed & Breakfast

PO Box 2369   221 E. Colorado Ave. *Telluride, CO 81435*   *(800) 338-7064*
Colleen & Tom Whiteman, Resident Owners   *(303) 728-6681*

LOCATION	Center of town, adjacent to Town Park & Historic Main Street
OPEN	All Year
DESCRIPTION	1982 Contemporary Victorian Contemporary furnishings
NO. OF ROOMS	8 w/private baths
RATES	$60-110 Reservation/cancellation policy Minimum stay during holidays & festivals
CREDIT CARDS	American Express, MasterCard, Visa
BREAKFAST	Full gourmet, served in dining room
AMENITIES	Cable TV/HBO, daily maid service, complimentary aprés ski & afternoon tea, sauna & steam room, central fireplace, roof top deck
RESTRICTIONS	No smoking. No pets. Children over 10
REVIEWED	*Colorado B&B Guide*
RSO	B&B Rocky Mountains Telluride Central Reservations
MEMBER	B&B Innkeepers of Colorado Colorado Hotel & Motel Assn.

THE DAHL HOUSE

PO Box 695   122 S. Oak   Telluride, CO 81435   (303) 728-4158
Mike & Christine Courter, Managers   FAX: (303) 728- 4158

LOCATION	Center of town, 1 block from ski lift
OPEN	Late May-Sept. & Thanksgiving-Early April
DESCRIPTION	1890's Victorian Antique furnishings
NO. OF ROOMS	1 w/private bath 8 w/shared baths
RATES	Summer/PB/$50-70 SB/$32-60 Winter/PB$60-75 SB/$40-65 Reservation/cancellation policy
CREDIT CARDS	American Express, MasterCard, Visa
BREAKFAST	Continental plus, served in dining room
AMENITIES	Parlor w/TV/games/books, apré ski in winter, discount ski packages arranged
RESTRICTIONS	Smoking limited. No pets (resident dog)
REVIEWED	*The Colorado Guide*
RSO	Telluride Central Reservations

THE JOHNSTONE INN

403 W. Colorado   PO Box 546   Telluride, CO 81435   (303) 728-3316
Bill Schiffbauer, Resident Owner   (800) 752-1901

LOCATION	Center of town, near ski lifts
OPEN	All Year
DESCRIPTION	1891 Victorian Victorian furnishings National Historic Register
NO. OF ROOMS	8 w/private baths
RATES	$70-150 Minimum stay during festivals & Christmas Reservation/cancellation policy

CREDIT CARDS	American Express, MasterCard, Visa
BREAKFAST	Full, served in dining room
AMENITIES	Hot tub, fresh flowers in rooms, phones, robes, laundry room, peaceful music, complimentary afternoon refreshments & extensive aprés ski in winter
RESTRICTIONS	No smoking. No pets. Children over 10

PENNINGTON'S MOUNTAIN VILLAGE INN

100 Pennington Court   PO Box 2428   Telluride, CO 81435
(303) 728-5337   FAX: (303) 728-5337
Michael & Judy Maclean, Resident Managers

LOCATION	Just outside Telluride. Stay on Hwy. 145 toward Ophir, turn right 2 mi. west of town, continue another 2-3 mi., turn left at our sign
OPEN	All Year
DESCRIPTION	Contemporary French Country On the 12th fairway of Telluride Golf Course Victorian furnishings
NO. OF ROOMS	12 w/private baths
RATES	$140-250 Reservation/cancellation policy
CREDIT CARDS	American Express, MasterCard, Visa
BREAKFAST	Full gourmet, served in dining room
AMENITIES	Complimentary happy hour, library lounge, indoor jacuzzi & steam room, game room w/TV, entry level lockers, laundry facilities, meeting facilities, handicapped access
RESTRICTIONS	No pets
AWARDS	Most Spectacular B&B Inn, B&B Rocky Mountains
REVIEWED	Colorado B&B Guide
RSO	B&B Rocky Mountains
MEMBER	Distinctive Inns of Colorado

THE SAN SOPHIA

PO Box 1825   330 W Pacific Ave.   Telluride, CO 81435   (303) 728-3001
Dianne & Gary Eschman, Resident Owners   (800) 537-4781

LOCATION	1/2 block from Oak St. ski lift
OPEN	Nov. 25-April 8 & May 7-Oct. 25
DESCRIPTION	1988 Contemporary Victorian Country furnishings
NO. OF ROOMS	16 w/private baths
RATES	Summer/$85-115 Winter/$125-175 5-night minimum during Christmas holiday Reservation/cancellation policy
CREDIT CARDS	American Express, MasterCard, Visa
BREAKFAST	Full gourmet buffet, served in dining room or on deck
AMENITIES	Complimentary extensive aprés ski, cable TV/VCR's/phones in rooms, robes, tubs for 2, covered parking, gazebo w/sunken jacuzzi, observatory, library/lounge w/fireplace, concierge service, English garden
RESTRICTIONS	No smoking. No pets. Children over 10
REVIEWED	*B&B American Style* *The Best B&B's & Country Inns* *Colorado B&B Guide* *Complete Guide to American B&B* *Complete Guide to B&B Inns & Guesthouses* *Fodor's Colorado* *Insider's Guide to the Best Skiing in Colorado* *Recommended Country Inns of the Rocky Mountain Region*
RSO	B&B Rocky Mountains Telluride Central Reservations
MEMBER	American B&B Assn. Distinctive Inns of Colorado
RATED	AAA 4 Diamonds ABBA 5 Crowns Mobil 4 Stars

244

TRINIDAD

This busy railroad and coalmining center is a straight shot south on I-25 from Denver, Colorado Springs and Pueblo, just 19 miles from the New Mexico border. The Corazon de Trinidad National Historic District is a charmer, and there are some good museums, too: Mitchell Memorial Museum & Gallery, Baca House, and Bloom Mansion. Trinidad Lake State Recreation Area is 3 miles west. Handy to Comanche National Grasslands.

BLUEHOUSE BED & BREAKFAST

824 W. Colorado Ave.   Trinidad, CO 81082   (719) 846-4507
Pam & Felix Panlasigui, Resident Owners

LOCATION	From I-25 Exit 14B, 6 blocks west on Colorado, 2 blocks from Trinidad State Junior College
OPEN	All Year
DESCRIPTION	1911 Victorian w/wrap-around porch Eclectic furnishings
NO. OF ROOMS	2 w/shared bath
RATES	$35-45 Reservations preferred
CREDIT CARDS	No
BREAKFAST	Full, served in dining room
AMENITIES	Fireplace in dining room, wrap-around porch, complimentary refreshments, off-street parking
RESTRICTIONS	No smoking. No pets (resident dogs & cat). Children over 3

TWIN LAKES

Once a mining camp, this tiny community sits at the foot of Mt. Elbert and Independence Pass, 20 miles southwest of Leadville on Hwy 24 and SR 82. Check out the mackinaw in Twin Lakes Reservoir, and the Annual Colorado vs. Texas Tomato War in September!

MT. ELBERT LODGE

PO Box 40   Hwy. 82   Twin Lakes, CO 81251   (719) 486-0594
Karen & Peter Rempel, Resident Managers

LOCATION	4-1/2 mi. west of Twin Lakes
OPEN	All Year
DESCRIPTION	2-Story Log Lodge Some antique & eclectic furnishings
NO. OF ROOMS	6 w/shared baths
RATES	$39-53 Reservation/cancellation policy
CREDIT CARDS	MasterCard, Visa
BREAKFAST	Continental plus, served in breakfast room
AMENITIES	Complimentary beverages, fireplace in common area, phone available
RESTRICTIONS	Smoking limited. No pets (resident dog & cat)
RSO	B&B Rocky Mountains

VAIL

In the Gore Creek Valley, 100 miles west of Denver on I-70, surrounded by three spectacular wilderness areas, this world-class resort is the largest ski complex in the U.S., famous for its back bowls and luxury. Summers are filled with concerts, celebrations, cultural and sporting events, and fall with VailFest. Gerald Ford is around a lot, too.

ALPEN HAUS

Through Reservation Service Only:
PO Box 491   Vail, CO 81658   (303) 949-1212   (800) 748-2666

LOCATION	At Golden Peak, 2 blocks east of Vail Village
OPEN	November-April
DESCRIPTION	1988 European Stucco European furnishings
NO. OF ROOMS	2 w/private baths
RATES	$105-125 Reservation/cancellation policy 2-night minimum in winter
CREDIT CARDS	MasterCard, Visa
BREAKFAST	Full, served in dining room
AMENITIES	TV/radio in rooms, complimentary refreshments
RESTRICTIONS	No smoking. No pets. No children
RSO	B&B Assn. of Vail/Ski Areas

ASPEN HAUS

Through Reservation Service Only:
PO Box 491   Vail, CO 81658   (303) 949-1212   (800) 748-2666

LOCATION	In West Vail, 2 mi. west of Vail Village
OPEN	November 1-April 15
DESCRIPTION	1978 European European furnishings
NO. OF ROOMS	1 w/private bath
RATES	$85-125 Reservation/cancellation policy 2-night minimum
CREDIT CARDS	MasterCard, Visa
BREAKFAST	Full, served in guestroom Dinner available by request
AMENITIES	TV/radio/phone in rooms, complimentary refreshments
RESTRICTIONS	No smoking. No pets (resident dog). No children
RSO	B&B Assn. of Vail/Ski Areas

THE ASPEN TREE

2614 Larkspur Ln.   Vail, CO 81657   (303) 479-9470
Agnes Miller, Resident Owner

LOCATION	South side of West Vail, 3 mi. from center of Vail
OPEN	Dec. 1-April 15 (Inquire about other dates)
DESCRIPTION	1990 Log Siding Country furnishings
NO. OF ROOMS	1 w/private bath 2 w/shared bath
RATES	PB/$100 SB/$75 Reservation/cancellation policy 2-night minimum stay

CREDIT CARDS	MasterCard, Visa
BREAKFAST	Full, served in guestrooms
AMENITIES	Robes, TV/radio in rooms, complimentary refreshments, on free bus route
RESTRICTIONS	No pets (resident dog)
RSO	B&B Assn. of Vail/Ski Areas

BLACK BEAR INN OF VAIL

2405 Elliott Rd.   Vail, CO 81657   (303) 476-1304
Jessie & David Edeen, Resident Owners

LOCATION	2 mi. west of Vail
OPEN	All Year
DESCRIPTION	1990 Handcrafted Log on Gore Creek Rustic furnishings
NO. OF ROOMS	12 w/private baths
RATES	$80-145 (Seasonal) Reservation/cancellation policy Inquire about minimum stays
CREDIT CARDS	MasterCard, Visa
BREAKFAST	Full gourmet, served in dining room
AMENITIES	Phone in rooms, sitting bays in most rooms, deck, antique stove in great room, complimentary refreshments, ski & boot storage, on free town bus route
RESTRICTIONS	No smoking. No pets (resident dog). Inquire about children
RSO	B&B Rocky Mountains Vail Resort Assn.
MEMBER	Distinctive Inns of Colorado

THE BLUE SPRUCE

2754 S. Frontage Rd.   Vail, CO 81657   (303) 479-0756
Darlene Schweinsberg & Rick Nibali, Resident Owners

LOCATION	South side of West Vail, 3 mi. from center of Vail
OPEN	Dec. 1-April 15 (Inquire about other dates)
DESCRIPTION	1965 Log Cabin On Gore Creek Country furnishings
NO. OF ROOMS	1 w/private bath 2 w/shared bath
RATES	PB/$125 SB/$100 Reservation/cancellation policy 2-night minimum
CREDIT CARDS	MasterCard, Visa (5% surcharge)
BREAKFAST	Full gourmet, served in guestrooms
AMENITIES	Hot tub by the creek, robes, TV/radio in rooms, phone available, complimentary afternoon refreshments & après ski, transportation from Eagle Airport, on free bus route
RESTRICTIONS	No pets (resident dog & cat)
RSO	B&B Assn. of Vail/Ski Areas

BLUEBIRD

Through Reservation Service Only:
PO Box 491   Vail, CO 81658   (303) 949-1212   (800) 748-2666

LOCATION	In West Vail, 3 mi. west of Vail Village
OPEN	All Year
DESCRIPTION	Mountain Chalet
NO. OF ROOMS	2 w/shared bath

RATES	Summer/$35-45 Winter/$65-85
	Reservation/cancellation policy
	2-night minimum in winter
CREDIT CARDS	MasterCard, Visa
BREAKFAST	Full, served in dining room
	Lunch available
AMENITIES	TV/radio in rooms, complimentary refreshments
RESTRICTIONS	No smoking. No pets. No children
RSO	B&B Assn. of Vail/Ski Areas

COLORADO COMFORT

Through Reservation Service Only:
PO Box 491   Vail, CO 81658   (303) 949-1212   (800) 748-2666

LOCATION	In Eagle-Vail
OPEN	All Year
DESCRIPTION	2-Story Contemporary
NO. OF ROOMS	1 w/private bath
RATES	Summer/$40-50 Winter/$75-85
	Reservation/cancellation policy
	2-night minimum
CREDIT CARDS	MasterCard, Visa
BREAKFAST	Full, served in dining room & guestrooms
AMENITIES	Robes, complimentary refreshments
RESTRICTIONS	No smoking. No pets. No children
RSO	B&B Assn. of Vail/Ski Areas

COLUMBINE CHALET
BED & BREAKFAST OF VAIL

PO Box 1407   Vail, CO 81658   (303) 476-1122   FAX: (303) 476-0102
Pat Funk, Resident Owner

LOCATION	Eastern edge of Vail Golf Course, on free Town of Vail bus route
OPEN	All Year
DESCRIPTION	1980 Austrian Chalet On Gore Creek Traditional furnishings
NO. OF ROOMS	3 w/private baths
RATES	Seasonal: $30-150 Reservation/cancellation policy Inquire about minimum stays & discount for extended stays & cash payments
CREDIT CARDS	MasterCard, Visa
BREAKFAST	Full, served in dining room or in guestrooms on request
AMENITIES	Hot tub on deck, robes, TV/radio in rooms, 1 room w/phone & fireplace, common phone for 2 rooms, books, games, fireplace & large screen TV in living room, complimentary afternoon refreshments, airport transportation & advance restaurant reservations arranged
RESTRICTIONS	No smoking. No pets (resident dog)
RSO	B&B Rocky Mountains B&B Assn. of Vail/Ski Areas

FAIRWAY HOUSE

Through Reservation Service Only:
PO Box 491   Vail, CO 81658   (303) 949-1212   (800) 748-2666

LOCATION	1/3 mi. from Golden Peak lifts
OPEN	October 31-April 31
DESCRIPTION	Contemporary Ranch
NO. OF ROOMS	1 w/private bath
RATES	Summer/$60-75 Winter/$90-125
	Reservation/cancellation policy
CREDIT CARDS	MasterCard, Visa
BREAKFAST	Full, served in dining room
AMENITIES	TV/radio/phone & fireplace in room
RESTRICTIONS	No pets (resident dog)
RSO	B&B Assn. of Vail/Ski Areas

KAY'S CORNER

Through Reservation Service Only:
PO Box 491   Vail, CO 81658   (303) 949-1212   (800) 748-2666

LOCATION	In West Vail, 5 mi. west of Vail Village
OPEN	All Year
DESCRIPTION	1982 Home
NO. OF ROOMS	2 w/private baths
RATES	$75-89
	Reservation/cancellation policy
	2-night minimum in winter
CREDIT CARDS	MasterCard, Visa
BREAKFAST	Full, served in dining room
AMENITIES	TV/radio/phone in rooms, complimentary après ski
RESTRICTIONS	No smoking. No pets (resident dog). Children over 12
RSO	B&B Assn. of Vail/Ski Areas

MATTERHORN

Through Reservation Service Only:
PO Box 491   Vail, CO 81658   (303) 949-1212   (800) 748-2666

LOCATION	In West Vail, 2 mi. west of Vail Village
OPEN	All Year
DESCRIPTION	1976 European European furnishings
NO. OF ROOMS	2 w/shared bath
RATES	Summer/$35-45 Winter/$65-79 Reservation/cancellation policy 2-night minimum in winter
CREDIT CARDS	MasterCard, Visa
BREAKFAST	Full, served in dining room Lunch available
AMENITIES	TV/radio/phone in rooms
RESTRICTIONS	No smoking. No pets (resident cat). Children over 12
RSO	B&B Assn. of Vail/Ski Areas

MOUNTAIN HIDEAWAY

Through Reservation Service Only:
PO Box 491   Vail, CO 86158   (303) 949-1212   (800) 748-2666

LOCATION	In East Vail, 5 mi. east of Vail Village
OPEN	All Year
DESCRIPTION	Contemporary Cabin
NO. OF ROOMS	2 w/private baths
RATES	Summer/$75-100 Winter/$85-125 Reservation/cancellation policy
CREDIT CARDS	MasterCard, Visa

BREAKFAST	Full, served in dining room
	Dinner available
AMENITIES	Hot tub/sauna, robes, TV/radio/phones in rooms
RESTRICTIONS	No smoking. No pets (resident cat & dog). Children over 12
RSO	B&B Assn. of Vail/Ski Areas

MRS. B'S

Through Reservation Service Only:
PO Box 491   Vail, CO 81658   (303) 949-1212   (800) 742-2666

LOCATION	1 mi. from Vail Village
OPEN	November 1-April 15
DESCRIPTION	Contemporary Duplex
	Contemporary furnishings
NO. OF ROOMS	1 w/private bath
RATES	$40-75
	Reservation/cancellation policy
	2-night minimum
CREDIT CARDS	MasterCard, Visa
BREAKFAST	Full, served in dining room or guestroom
AMENITIES	TV/radio/phone in rooms, complimentary refreshments
RESTRICTIONS	No smoking. No pets (resident dog). No children
RSO	B&B Assn. of Vail/Ski Areas

SIS'S

Through Reservation Service Only:
PO Box 491   Vail, CO 81658   (303) 949-1212   (800) 748-2666

LOCATION	West Vail
OPEN	November 15-May 1
DESCRIPTION	2-Story Townhome Southwestern furnishings
NO. OF ROOMS	2 w/shared bath
RATES	Summer/$35-45 Winter/$70-80 Reservation/cancellation policy
CREDIT CARDS	MasterCard, Visa
BREAKFAST	Full or continental, served in dining room
AMENITIES	TV/radio/phone in rooms, complimentary refreshments
RESTRICTIONS	No smoking. No pets. No children
RSO	B&B Assn. of Vail/Ski Areas

SPORTSMAN'S HAVEN

Through Reservation Service Only:
PO Box 491   Vail, CO 81658   (303) 949-1212   (800) 748-2666

LOCATION	In East Vail, 5 mi. east of Vail Village
OPEN	All Year
DESCRIPTION	Contemporary Home Sporting interior
NO. OF ROOMS	2 w/private baths
RATES	Summer/$40-45 Winter/$65-85 Reservation/cancellation policy
CREDIT CARDS	MasterCard, Visa

BREAKFAST	Full, served in dining room Lunch available
AMENITIES	TV/radio in rooms, complimentary refreshments
RESTRICTIONS	No smoking. No pets (resident dog). Children over 10
RSO	B&B Assn. of Vail/Ski Areas

Streamside

Through Reservation Service Only:
PO Box 491   Vail, CO 81658   (303) 949-1212   (800) 748-2666

LOCATION	2 mi. west of Vail Village
OPEN	All Year
DESCRIPTION	1980 Home Rustic furnishings
NO. OF ROOMS	2 w/shared bath
RATES	Summer/$40 Winter/$65 Reservation/cancellation policy 2-night minimum
CREDIT CARDS	MasterCard, Visa
BREAKFAST	Full, served in dining room Lunch available
AMENITIES	TV/radio in rooms, complimentary refreshments
RESTRICTIONS	No smoking. No pets (resident dog). Children over 12
RSO	B&B Assn. of Vail/Ski Areas

VAIL VIEW BED & BREAKFAST

Through Reservation Service Only:
PO Box 491   Vail, CO 81658   (303) 949-1212   (800) 748-2666

LOCATION	1.5 mi. west of Vail Village
OPEN	All Year
DESCRIPTION	2-Story Townhome Casual furnishings
NO. OF ROOMS	1 w/private bath
RATES	Summer/$50-53 Winter/$70-75 Reservation/cancellation policy 2-night minimum
CREDIT CARDS	MasterCard, Visa
BREAKFAST	Full, served in dining room Lunch available
AMENITIES	TV/radio/phone in room, complimentary refreshments
RESTRICTIONS	No smoking. No pets (resident cat). No children
RSO	B&B Assn. of Vail/Ski Areas

VILLAGE ARTIST

Through Reservation Service Only:
PO Box 491   Vail, CO 81658   (303) 949-1212   (800) 748-2666

LOCATION	In Vail Village
OPEN	All Year
DESCRIPTION	Contemporary Home
NO. OF ROOMS	2 w/shared bath

RATES	Summer/$30-45 Winter/$75-85
	Reservation/cancellation policy
CREDIT CARDS	MasterCard, Visa
BREAKFAST	Full, served in dining room
AMENITIES	TV/radio in rooms
RESTRICTIONS	No smoking. No pets. No children
RSO	B&B Assn. of Vail/Ski Areas

WHISKEY HILL

Through Reservation Service Only:
PO Box 491   Vail, CO 81658   (303) 949-1212   (800) 748-2666

LOCATION	Half-way between Vail & Beaver Creek
OPEN	October 31-May 1
DESCRIPTION	Lock-Off Condo
NO. OF ROOMS	1 w/private bath
RATES	Summer/$45-60 Winter/$80-85
	Reservation/cancellation policy
	2-night minimum
CREDIT CARDS	MasterCard, Visa
BREAKFAST	Full, served in guestroom
AMENITIES	TV/radio/phone & fireplace in room
RESTRICTIONS	No smoking. No pets. Children over 12
RSO	B&B Assn. of Vail/Ski Areas

VICTOR
(CRIPPLE CREEK)

50 miles southwest of Colorado Springs, this gold-mining boom town is part of the Cripple Creek-Victor National Historic District. The Lowell Thomas Museum tells about its most famous resident. Handy to gambling in Cripple Creek.

THE KESSEY HOUSE

212 S. 3rd St.   PO Box 113   Victor, CO 80860   (719) 689-2235
Carol & Robert James, Resident Owners

LOCATION	Center of town, 1-1/2 blocks south of 3rd St. & Victor Ave. intersection
OPEN	All Year
DESCRIPTION	1899 2-Story Victorian Victorian & eclectic furnishings
NO. OF ROOMS	4 w/shared baths
RATES	$35-45
CREDIT CARDS	MasterCard, Visa
BREAKFAST	Full, served in dining room
RESTRICTIONS	Smoking & pets limited

THE PORTLAND INN

412 W. Portland Ave.   PO Box 32   Victor, CO 80860   (719) 689-2102
Guido & Sandy Honeycutt, Resident Owners

LOCATION	Center of town, 1 block off main street
OPEN	All Year
DESCRIPTION	1898 Victorian Victorian furnishings National Historic Register
NO. OF ROOMS	1 w/private bath 3 w/shared baths
RATES	PB/$65-75 SB/$35-55 Reservation/cancellation policy
CREDIT CARDS	American Express, Discover, MasterCard, Visa
BREAKFAST	Continental plus, served in dining room
AMENITIES	Outdoor hot tub, decks, private guest area, crib
RESTRICTIONS	Smoking limited. Resident dog & cat
REVIEWED	*Recommended Country Inns of the Rocky Mountain Region*
RSO	B&B Rocky Mountains
MEMBER	B&B Innkeepers of Colorado

WHEAT RIDGE
(DENVER)

A western suburb of Denver, off I-70 exit 269. Check out the Wheat Ridge Sod House & Museum.

ALLISON MANOR

3270 Allison St.   Wheat Ridge, CO 80033   (303) 232-1002
Donna & Jack Bailey, Resident Owners

LOCATION	2 mi. south of I-70, Exit 269A. Hwy 121 south to 32nd Ave, west 1/4 mi. to Allison
OPEN	All Year
DESCRIPTION	1985 2-Story Ranch
NO. OF ROOMS	2 w/private baths
RATES	$40-55 Reservation/cancellation policy
CREDIT CARDS	MasterCard, Visa
BREAKFAST	Full, served in dining room
AMENITIES	Hot tub, complimentary refreshments, sitting room w/TV/puzzles/games/books
RESTRICTIONS	No smoking. No pets. Children under 14

WINTER PARK
(INCLUDES FRASER)

Owned by the City of Denver, this is a major ski resort with three interconnected mountains in the Fraser Valley. Check out the summer music festivals and mountain bike events. From Denver, 67 miles northwest via I-70 and Hwy. 40, or try the Denver & Rio Grande Ski Train on winter weekends. Fraser, 2 miles north of Winter Park on Hwy. 40, is proudly known as the "The Icebox of the Nation."

ALPEN ROSE BED & BREAKFAST

---

244 Forest Trail   PO Box 769   Winter Park, CO 80482   (303) 726-5039
Robin & Rupert Sommerauer, Resident Owners

LOCATION	Left on Vasquez to Forest Trail Rd., right on Forest Trail
OPEN	All Year
DESCRIPTION	1950 Mountain Home Austrian furnishings
NO. OF ROOMS	5 w/private baths
RATES	$55-95 Reservation/cancellation policy
CREDIT CARDS	American Express, MasterCard, Visa
BREAKFAST	Full gourmet, served in common room
AMENITIES	Hot tub, deck, complimentary fresh-baked Austrian pastries & refreshments, fireplace in common area, free shuttle bus service from front door, handicapped access
RESTRICTIONS	No smoking. No pets (resident cat & hamster). Children over 10
REVIEWED	*Colorado B&B Guide*
RSO	Winter Park Central Reservations
MEMBER	B&B Innkeepers of Colorado

AngelMark Bed & Breakfast

50 Little Pierre Ave.   PO Box 161   Winter Park, CO 80482
(303) 726-5354   (800) 424-2158
Bob & Jeanenne Temple, Resident Owners

LOCATION	4 mi. west of Winter Park in Winter Park Ranch subdivision
OPEN	All Year
DESCRIPTION	1979 Mountain Home Eclectic furnishings
NO. OF ROOMS	3 w/private baths
RATES	$75-95 Reservation/cancellation policy
CREDIT CARDS	MasterCard, Visa
BREAKFAST	Full gourmet, served in dining area
AMENITIES	Hot tub/sauna, robes, TV/radio & fireplaces in some rooms, complimentary hors d'oeuvres, small meeting facilities, computer & FAX services available
RESTRICTIONS	No smoking. No pets. No children
RSO	Winter Park Central Reservations
MEMBER	B&B Innkeepers of Colorado B&B of Winter Park

BEAU WEST BED & BREAKFAST

148 Fir Drive   PO Box 3156   Winter Park, CO 80482   (303) 726-5145
Susan Mutersbaugh & Greg Baca, Resident Owners   (800) 473-5145

LOCATION	500 yds. from base of Winter Park ski area
OPEN	June-April
DESCRIPTION	1990 Remodeled Modern Modern w/some antique furnishings
NO. OF ROOMS	2 w/private baths 1 w/shared bath
RATES	Summer/$55 Winter/$95 Reservation/cancellation policy Inquire about minimum stays
CREDIT CARDS	MasterCard, Visa
BREAKFAST	Full, served in dining room
AMENITIES	Hot tub, robes, radio & phone in rooms, TV/VCR/stereo & fireplace in common room, train station transportation
RESTRICTIONS	No smoking. No pets (resident cat). Children over 2
REVIEWED	*Fodor's Skiing in the U.S.A. & Canada*
MEMBER	B&B of Winter Park

265

CHALET ZIRBISEGGER
BED & BREAKFAST

115 County Rd. 716   PO Box 15   Winter Park, CO 80482
Ewald & Candace Zirbisegger, Resident Owners   (303) 726-5416

LOCATION	In Old Town Winter Park, 600 yds. from base of Winter Park Resort
OPEN	Nov. 15-April 15 & June 1-Sept. 30
DESCRIPTION	Rustic Mountain Lodge Southwestern furnishings
NO. OF ROOMS	8 w/private baths
RATES	$60-90 Reservation/cancellation policy 5-night minimum during Christmas holiday
CREDIT CARDS	MasterCard, Visa
BREAKFAST	Full buffet, served in dining room Sack lunches available at extra charge
AMENITIES	Ski-in access to front door, outdoor hot tub/sauna, TV in game room, fireplace in living room, complimentary refreshments, meeting facilities, ski-tuning, free shuttle service
RESTRICTIONS	Smoking limited. No pets (resident dog)
RSO	Winter Park Central Reservations

ENGELMANN PINES

1035 Cranmer Ave.   PO Box 1305   Winter Park, CO 80482
(800) 992-9512   (303) 726-4632
Margaret & Heinz Engel, Resident Owners

LOCATION	Right at stop light at Safeway Center, 1/2 mi. to Cranmer Ave, 1/2 mi. to right
OPEN	All Year
DESCRIPTION	1984 Contemporary Mountain European & American antique furnishings
NO. OF ROOMS	2 w/private baths 4 w/shared baths
RATES	PB/$65-95 SB/$55-85 Reservation/cancellation policy
CREDIT CARDS	American Express, MasterCard, Visa
BREAKFAST	Full gourmet, served in dining room
AMENITIES	Jacuzzi tubs in some rooms, robes, down comforters & pillows, radio in rooms, portable phone, fireplace in 1 room & common room, TV/VCR in common room, guest kitchen, complimentary refreshments, small meeting facilities, train station transporation, free shuttle bus
RESTRICTIONS	No smoking. No pets (resident dogs). Inquire about children
REVIEWED	*B&B U.S.A.* *Colorado B&B Guide*
RSO	B&B Rocky Mountains
MEMBER	B&B Innkeepers of Colorado B&B of Winter Park

IVER'S SVENKA

210 Fraser Ave.   Fraser, CO 80442   (303) 796-8669
Mailing address: 7434 S. Monroe Court   Littleton, CO 80122
Jody & Skeeter Gingery, Owners

LOCATION	2 mi. west of Winter Park village, 1 block off Hwy. 40
OPEN	All Year
DESCRIPTION	1928 Renovated Swedish Pioneer's Home Contemporary Swedish furnishings
NO. OF ROOMS	3-bedroom guesthouse w/shared bath Accommodates 1-10 persons
RATES	Whole house: 1-3/$105 4-6/$150 7-10/$195 11+/$6 per additional person Reservation/cancellation policy
CREDIT CARDS	No
BREAKFAST	Swedish continental, served in dining room
AMENITIES	Cable TV, radio, portable phone, fully equipped kitchen, small meeting facilities, handicapped access
RESTRICTIONS	No pets

KAREN'S BED & BREAKFAST

54 Icicle Way   PO Box 682   Fraser, CO 80442   (303) 726-9398
Karen Newton & Steve Morrow, Resident Owners

LOCATION	2 mi. west of Fraser in Ice Box Estates, 7 mi. from Winter Park
OPEN	All Year
DESCRIPTION	1982 2-Story Natural Cedar Contemporary furnishings

NO. OF ROOMS	2 w/shared baths
RATES	Summer/$40-60 Winter/$50-70 2-night minimum
CREDIT CARDS	No
BREAKFAST	Full, served in dining room
AMENITIES	Robes, complimentary refreshments
RESTRICTIONS	No smoking. No pets (resident dog). Children 12 & over
RSO	Winter Park/Fraser Valley Chamber
MEMBER	B&B of Winter Park

MULLIGAN'S MOUNTAIN INN

148 Fern Way   PO Box 397   Winter Park, CO 80482   (303) 887-2877
Shirley & Fred Mulligan, Resident Owners

LOCATION	3 mi. north of Tabernash, 10 mi. north of Winter Park
OPEN	Jan. 1-May 1 & June 1-Dec. 31
DESCRIPTION	1982 2-Story Contemporary Contemporary furnishings
NO. OF ROOMS	4 w/shared baths Loft available
RATES	$35-85 Reservation/cancellation policy
CREDIT CARDS	No
BREAKFAST	Full, served in dining room
AMENITIES	Outdoor jacuzzi, TV/radio/phone in living room, complimentary fruit basket & refreshments, game room w/pool table, darts, Nintendo
RESTRICTIONS	No smoking. No pets (resident dog). Children over 10
RSO	Winter Park Central Reservations
MEMBER	National B&B Assn.

Nordic Bed & Breakfast

150 Eisenhower Ave.   PO Box 759   Fraser, CO 80442   (303) 726-8459
Eileen Waldow & Family, Resident Owners

LOCATION	2 mi. north of Winter Park, 2 blocks off Hwy. 40, 1/2 block from Amtrack station
OPEN	All Year
NO. OF ROOMS	4 w/shared baths
RATES	$35-43 Reservation/cancellation policy
CREDIT CARDS	No
BREAKFAST	Full, served in dining room Special diets available
AMENITIES	Ski wax bench, bike stand, handicapped access
RESTRICTIONS	No smoking. Inquire about pets (resident dog)

The Outpost Inn

687 County Rd. 517   PO Box 41   Winter Park, CO 80482
Susie & Jerry Frye, Resident Owners   (303) 726-5346

LOCATION	2.8 mi. west of Hwy. 40, 1/2 mi. north of Fraser
OPEN	Dec.-April 15
DESCRIPTION	1977 2-Story Western Frame Danish furnishings
NO. OF ROOMS	7 w/private baths
RATES	$55-90 Reservation/cancellation policy

CREDIT CARDS	No
BREAKFAST	Full gourmet, served in dining room Dinner available at extra charge
AMENITIES	Hot tub/sauna, radio in rooms, complimentary aprés ski, fireplace in common room, evening ski films, ski area transportation, free shuttle bus, limited handicapped access
RESTRICTIONS	No smoking. No pets (resident critters: cat, dog, canary, llamas)
RSO	B&B Rocky Mountains Winter Park Central Reservations

THE QUILTED BEAR

1709 County Rd. 83   PO Box 1020   Winter Park, CO 80482
(303) 726-5084   FAX: (303) 726-5084
Cindy & John Augustin, Resident Owners

LOCATION	8 mi. north of Winter Park Ski Area on Hwy. 40, 2 mi. east on County Rd. 83 (Devil's Thumb Rd.)
OPEN	Nov. 15-April 5 & July-Sept.
DESCRIPTION	1981 Mountain Home on 10 acres
NO. OF ROOMS	5 w/private baths
RATES	$60-85 Reservation/cancellation policy 5-night minimum during Christmas holiday
CREDIT CARDS	No
BREAKFAST	Full, served in dining room
AMENITIES	Hot tub/sauna, complimentary refreshments
RESTRICTIONS	No smoking. No pets. Children over 10
MEMBER	B&B of Winter Park

271

SOMETHING SPECIAL

1848 County Rd. 83   PO Box 800   Winter Park, CO 80482
Noël Wilson, Resident Owner   (303) 726-5360

LOCATION	8 mi. north of Winter Park Ski Area on Hwy. 40, 2 mi. east on County Rd. 83 (Devil's Thumb Rd.)
OPEN	All Year
DESCRIPTION	1965 Ranch On 14 acres Antique & country furnishings
NO. OF ROOMS	1 w/private bath 2 w/shared bath
RATES	Summer/PB/$55-65 SB/$45-55 Winter/PB/$65-75 SB/$55-65 Reservation/cancellation policy
CREDIT CARDS	American Express for reservations only
BREAKFAST	Full, served in dining room
AMENITIES	Robes, down comforters, complimentary refreshments, handicapped access
RESTRICTIONS	No smoking. No pets (resident cat, dog, horses) No children
MEMBER	B&B of Winter Park

WOODLAND PARK
(COLORADO SPRINGS)

A growing mountain community 25 miles northwest of Colorado Springs on Hwy. 24. It's close to Manitou Lake and Rampart Reservoir, and handy to Florissant Fossil Beds National Monument, Tarryall & Eleven Mile Reservoirs.

HACKMAN HOUSE BED & BREAKFAST

---

602 W. Midland Ave. PO Box 6902 Woodland Park, CO 80866
Laurie Glauth & Jan Greene, Resident Owners (719) 687-9851

LOCATION	1 block west of Dairy Queen on corner of Elm & Midland
OPEN	All Year
DESCRIPTION	1887 2-Story Victorian Native American & Country Victorian furnishings
NO. OF ROOMS	2 w/private baths 2 w/shared bath
RATES	PB/$67-85 SB/$57-75 Reservation/cancellation policy
CREDIT CARDS	MasterCard, Visa
BREAKFAST	Full, served in dining room
AMENITIES	Radio in rooms, TV in common area, fireplaces in 2 rooms & parlor, library, complimentary evening refreshments, therapeutic massage available, meeting facilities
RESTRICTIONS	No smoking. No pets. No children
MEMBER	B&B Innkeepers of Colorado

PIKES PEAK PARADISE
BED & BREAKFAST

236 Pinecrest Rd.   PO Box 5760   Woodland Park, CO 80866-5760
(719) 687-6656   (800) 728-8282
Tim Stoddard, Martin Meier & Priscilla Arthur, Resident Owners

LOCATION	3 mi. west of Woodland Park, off Trout Creek Rd.
OPEN	All Year
DESCRIPTION	1988 2-Story Greek Revival/Georgian (Southern Plantation) Traditional furnishings
NO. OF ROOMS	5 w/private baths
RATES	$85-110 Reservation/cancellation policy
CREDIT CARDS	American Express, Discover, MasterCard, Visa
BREAKFAST	Full gourmet, served in dining room or guestrooms
AMENITIES	Hot tub, fireplaces in rooms, private entrances, patio, complimentary refreshments, small meeting facilities, handicapped access
RESTRICTIONS	No smoking. No pets (resident dogs). Children 12 & over
RSO	B&B Rocky Mountains

YELLOW JACKET
(CORTEZ)

This agricultural area 15 miles northwest of Cortez on Hwy. 666, has one of the most scenic and important Anasazi archaeological sites in the southwest. Check out the Yellow Jacket Ruin west of Yellow Jacket Canyon and Creek. There's no town here, so look for the historic Post Office.

WILSON'S PINTO BEAN FARM

PO Box 252   Yellow Jacket, CO 81335   (303) 562-4476
Esther M. & Arthur Wilson, Resident Owners

LOCATION	From Hwy. 666, turn left on Road Y, then 1/2 mi. south on Road 16
OPEN	April-October
DESCRIPTION	1946 Farmhouse on 1200 acres Country furnishings Working pinto bean farm
NO. OF ROOMS	1 w/private bath 1 w/shared bath
RATES	$30-33 Reservation/cancellation policy
CREDIT CARDS	No
BREAKFAST	Full, served in dining room Supper available at extra charge
AMENITIES	TV/radio, large deck
RESTRICTIONS	No smoking
REVIEWED	*Birnbaum's Farm & Ranch Vacations*

INDEX